Amongst the Sikhs

Amongst the Sikhs: Reaching for the Stars

Other Titles

Claudia Preckel	*Begums of Bhopal*
Dhananjaya Singh	*The House of Marwar*
E. Jaiwant Paul	*Baji Rao: The Warrior Peshwa*
E. Jaiwant Paul	*Rani of Jhansi: Lakshmi Bai*
Girish Chaturvedi	*Tansen*
Indira Menon	*The Madras Quartet: Women in Karnatak Music*
Irene Frain	*Phoolan*
Jagdish Chander Wadhawan	*Manto Naama: The Life of Saadat Hasan Manto*
Jeannine Auboyer	*Buddha*
John Lall	*Begam Samru: Fading Portrait in a Gilded Frame*
Jyoti Jafa	*Nurjahan*
K.M. George	*The Best of Thakazhi Sivasankara Pillai*
Maj. Gen. Ian Cardozo	*Param Vir: Our Heroes in Battle*
Namita Gokhale	*Mountain Echoes: Reminiscences of Kumaoni Women*
Neelima Dalmia Adhar	*Father Dearest: The Life and Times of R.K. Dalmia*
Nina Epton	*Beloved Empress: Mumtaz Mahal*
Rachel Dwyer	*Yash Chopra: Fifty Years in Indian Cinema*
Ralph Russel	*The Famous Ghalib*
Rashna Imhasly-Gandhi	*Psychology of Love: Wisdom of Indian Mythology*
Savita Devi	*Maa . . . Siddheshwari*
Sumati Mutatkar	*Shrikrishna Narayan Ratanjankar 'Sujan'*
V.S. Naravane (ed.)	*Devdas and Other Stories* by Sarat Chandra Chatterji

Amongst the Sikhs

Reaching for the Stars

Dr Surjit Kaur

Introduction

Khushwant Singh

Lotus Collection

This edition first published in 2003
The Lotus Collection
An imprint of
Roli Books Pvt. Ltd.
M-75, G.K. II Market
New Delhi 110 048
Phones: ++91 (011) 2921 2271, 2921 2782
2921 0886, Fax: ++91 (011) 2921 7185
E-mail: roli@vsnl.com; Website: rolibooks.com
Also at
Varanasi, Agra, Jaipur and the Netherlands

ISBN: 81-7436-267-3
Rs 595

Typeset in Minion by Roli Books Pvt. Ltd. and
printed at Tan Prints India Pvt. Ltd., Haryana

Contents

This book is dedicated to my father
the Late Sardar Jodh Singh
(formerly of All India Radio, Jalandhar)
who spent his entire life spreading the message of
Guru Nanak.

Sardar Jodh Singh
(1911–1993)

Dr Surjit Kaur, the author, with Khushwant Singh, her guide and mentor.

Introduction

The landing of the first men on the moon in July 1969 is the subject of a popular joke amongst the Sikhs. As the American astronauts Neil Armstrong and Edwin Aldrin set foot on the lunar soil, who did they run into but a Sardarji family out for an evening stroll.

Armstrong and Aldrin asked them in utter amazement, 'When on earth did you get here?'

'We decided to come and settle here when we left Pakistan following the Partition of India in 1947,' replied the head of the family.

The joke is meant to illustrate the fact that no matter where you go in the world, you are sure to run into a handful of Sikhs. Out of an estimated population of around 19 million, well over a million Sikhs live in foreign lands.

Sikh emigration began during the British rule in India. In the course of the two Anglo-Sikh wars in 1845 and 1849, the English got a taste of Sikh prowess. After defeating and annexing their kingdoms, the British recruited Sikhs in large numbers for the British Indian Army. Thereafter, whenever the British were engaged in hostilities, Sikh soldiers constituted the vanguard. The British also recruited Sikhs in sizeable numbers for the police. To date Sikhs are known as Bengalis in Burma (Myanmar) because the first batch to be sent there hailed from the Bengal police. Sikh soldiers and policemen were also dispatched to Hong Kong, Singapore and Malaysia. On retirement many of them decided to settle in these countries. And their sons ventured out to yet other countries. Some headed for Thailand and the Philippines, while others settled in Australia and became farmers.

Woolooga, a village north of Brisbane, is largely populated by Sikhs growing avocado pears and bananas. The village has two gurdwaras. In one of them, the *Guru ka langar* is equipped with a bar to serve beer and spirits after the evening service. A few Sikhs found their way to New Zealand, and some became cattle-breeders. In one cattle farm I saw a huge but aged stud bull roaming around the house. The lady of the house explained, 'We have not sold him because he fathered most of our prize-winning cows and bulls. He is one of the family, and the founder of our fortunes. We call him Sardar Bahadur.'

During the same period, Sikhs began to migrate to British colonies on the West Coast of Africa, mainly Kenya and Uganda. Unlike other migrants who were largely agriculturists, most of those who went to Africa were craftsmen, entrepreneurs and professionals: mechanics, carpenters, doctors, engineers, teachers and the like. In the 1970s the cannibal dictator Idi Amin grabbed power and drove Indians out of Uganda. At the same time the well-being of Indians bred a lot of resentment amongst black Kenyans. Increasingly ill at ease in Kenya, Indians migrated in large numbers to England and other European countries.

Sikhs from Africa are still distinguishable from the style in which they wear their white turbans.

There was yet another wave of Sikh emigration comprising mainly agricultural workers and building contractors from Punjab to the Arab countries of the Middle East and North Africa. Those who could cross immigration barriers managed to get to Europe. An example of their grit is the existence of a small colony of Sikh farmers in villages a short distance from Milan.

How many of these Sikh émigrés have been able to conform to the Khalsa tradition of unshorn hair and unshaved beards? Have their second and third generations been able to conform to these diktats? What impact have events in their homeland like the demand for a separate sovereign Sikh State (Khalistan), had on them? These are some of the questions which Dr Surjit Kaur, a qualified sociologist based in Washington DC has tried to answer through extensive interviews of a cross-section of Sikhs settled in the United States, England, Canada and Australia.

With his distinctive turban and beard, a Sikh stands out in a crowd. Yet there is a lot of disinformation about the Sikh faith and way of life. A recent example of such ignorance was the eruption of xenophobia in North America following the bombing of the World Trade Center in New York City, and the attack on the Pentagon in Washington DC on Tuesday, 11 September 2001. Hoodlums picked on Sikhs in the belief that they were Arab Muslims and, therefore, supporters of Osama bin Laden. One Sikh was shot dead in Arizona.

Having lived abroad off and on from the early 1930s, I have had many amusing experiences of a mistaken identity. In my student days in England, I was mistaken either for a magician or a Maharaja. In Canada I was a Red Indian who wrapped feathers under a piece of cloth, instead of wearing them on his head. The most amusing experience, however, was in Jerusalem. In the hotel dining room I found myself seated next to an American-Jewish couple on a pilgrimage to their Holy Land. They were puzzled by my appearance. After some hesitation the man turned to me and said, 'Sir, forgive my intrusion. My wife Ruth and I were wondering where you may be from.'

I decided to have some fun at their expense and replied, 'I'll give you three guesses.'

After a pause the wife ventured, 'You wouldn't be Jewish, would you?'

'No, I am not a Jew.'

'How could he be Jewish?' scolded her husband. 'Does he look like a Jew? Maybe you are a Muscleman.'

'No, I am not a Mussalman.'

'Buddhist?'

'No, I am not even a Buddhist.'

They could not think of another religion or nationality. 'We give up. Please tell us who you are?'

'I am a Sikh,' I replied.

'That's the same as Sheikh. Aren't Sheikhs Musclemen?'

'Not Sheikh, but Sikh. We are not Mussalmans.'

'Ah!' said the man triumphantly, 'Then you must be from Sikkim.'

I threw up my hands in despair, abandoning all attempts to educate them. The man told me he had a nice laundry business in New York. It was understandable that he knew nothing about Sikhs. What would an Indian dhobi know about Jews?

Now for a few words about the genesis of this unique community, what it believes in and why it looks different from all others.

The word 'Sikh' is derived from the Sanskrit '*shishya*' meaning disciple. Sikhs are disciples of ten Gurus or teachers—from Guru Nanak (1469–1539) to Guru Gobind Singh (d 1708). Their faith is enshrined in their holy book, the *Guru Granth Sahib*, compiled in 1603 by Guru Arjan, their fifth Guru, who was later arrested, and tortured to death on the orders of the Mughal Governor of Lahore. The *Guru Granth Sahib* comprises over 6000 hymns set to the ragas of Indian classical music. It contains writings of the first five Gurus to which the last Guru added compositions of his father, Guru Tegh Bahadur, who was executed by the Mughal authorities in Delhi in AD 1675. The *Guru Granth Sahib* is perhaps the only truly eclectic religious scripture, as it also includes compositions of Hindu and Muslim poet-saints of the time. A Sikh is defined as one who believes in the ten Gurus, the *Guru Granth Sahib*, and does not subscribe to any other religion.

Sikhs are monotheists. They believe in the one formless and unperishable God, who is the Supreme Truth. They do not subscribe to idol worship or the caste system. They do not accept exclusivism or celibacy as a means to achieve godhead, and believe goodness should be achieved by living with one's family and as a member of society. In Guru Nanak's words: 'Work, share some of what you have earned, take the name of the Lord.'

After the martyrdom of their fifth and ninth Gurus, Sikhism underwent a radical change. While sticking to the tenets of Guru Nanak, Guru Gobind Singh decided to take up arms in defense of his faith. 'When all other means have failed, it is righteous to draw the sword,' he said. In AD 1699 he called on his followers to constitute a fraternity named the Khalsa or the Pure. He made them take vows, which included, amongst other things, to never cut their hair or shave their beards. This was customary amongst his predecessors and certain sects of sadhus: he wanted to create an army of soldier-saints. All of them were given the surname Singh (lion) to signify that they all belonged to a family sans cast. He himself changed his name from Gobind Rai to Gobind Singh.

In his battles against the Mughals, Gobind Singh lost all his four sons. He declared the end of the succession of the Gurus, and established the *Guru Granth Sahib* as the symbolic representation of the ten Gurus. Guru Gobind Singh was assassinated by two of his Pathan Muslim retainers at Nanded (Maharashtra) in 1708.

Although Guru Gobind Singh did not win any spectacular

victories, he infused his followers with a spirit of daredevilry which helped them oust the Mughals from Punjab, and by the end of the eighteenth century set up a kingdom of their own under Maharaja Ranjit Singh (AD 1780–1839). The kingdom disintegrated soon after his death, and after the two wars in 1845 and 1869, was annexed by the British.

Sikhs have two parallel traditions. Their theology remains the same as enshrined in the *Guru Granth Sahib* and is largely based on the *Upanishads.* Alongside runs the tradition of the militant Khalsa conceived by Guru Gobind Singh. Some of the never-say-die spirit, which they inherited from the Guru, survives in the form of enterprise and one-upmanship. In a country teeming with beggars, you will never see a Sikh begging for alms.

This collection of profiles of Sikhs is entirely the work of Dr Surjit Kaur, carried out under my guidance and with my collaboration. We felt strongly that the story of Sikhs living away from their homeland, striking roots in alien soils and yet retaining their distinct identity, needed to be told. We have done our best to tell it.

—*Khushwant Singh*

Note to the Reader

Ever since I migrated to the United States and took up American citizenship it had been on my mind that the last I had published was in the 1970s. The itch to write, however, remained. I was eager to resume writing and got the opportunity to do so after I came to know Sardar Khushwant Singh. This project was conceived over the phone during one of those routine conversations (night here in Washington DC and *amrit vela* in New Delhi). I told him that I wanted to return to India to do some fieldwork in Punjab that he could write about once I was through. The idea appealed to him. At the same time, he suggested an alternative project—I write on the hundreds of thousands of Sikhs settled abroad.

They came in search of opportunities and succeeded despite all odds. They looked different. Jobs were difficult to come by and neighbours regarded them with suspicion. Some gave up the outward emblems of their faith, others upheld their traditions, striving to overcome the prejudices of an alien people.

Sardar Khushwant Singh suggested a list of questions and a framework for interviews to be conducted amongst a cross-section of Sikhs living in North America and other Western countries. I selected over thirty Sikh families for my research. Inevitably interviewing those who had made a name for themselves or built a fortune seemed a more attractive proposition. Availability of such people was the next consideration. Since I had set aside only one week for fieldwork in London, I could not meet Reuben Singh—an icon of Sikh youth in London. In Canada while I was able to interview Gurbax Singh Malhi, the only turbaned Sikh Member of Parliament, who had assumed office on 25 October 1993, I could not contact Herb Dhaliwal who became a Minister in the Federal Government, nor Ujjal Dosanjh who became Prime Minister of British Columbia.

Year before last, I interviewed Sikh families from my hometown—Falls Church, Virginia—and those living in the neighbouring areas. All of them had to battle heavy odds in the beginning, but always kept up their 'Khalsa Spirit'. Often they were homesick; they missed their families left behind in Punjab, and wept each time a call or a letter apprised them of the death of a dear one.

In Canada, Gurdeep Singh Saluja—my younger brother Harjit's classmate and a friend—drew up a list of prominent Sikhs living in Toronto. Heading the list was Gurbax Singh Malhi, a Khalsa and Member of Parliament who had set out one day from a village in district Moga of Punjab. Then there was a lawyer and journalist T-Sher Singh, an internationally known wrestler, Tigarjit Singh and many others.

In London, Daya Singh Aulakh and Piara Singh Aulakh who had witnessed the Sikh community grow by leaps and bounds since the 1950s introduced me to Sikh Members of Parliament, businessmen, Queen's Counsellors, journalists and others who had made their mark in their adopted country. Sardar Gurmukh Singh, a retired Civil Servant gave me a lot of material and articles published on his talented brother Dya Singh in Australia.

My trip to California was made possible by Gurbax Kaur Kahlon who drove me to Yuba City and set up an interview with Dr Narinder Singh Kapany and his wife. At the Kapanys' home I saw some rare paintings including one of Rani Jindan by an English artist, Sobha Singh's portrait of Guru Nanak and Arpana Kaur's *Sohni-Mahiwal.* Dr Kapany, a distinguished scientist came to California in 1950. Ever since he has lived by the conviction: 'Don't let anyone tell you that being a Sikh is a disadvantage. I never had to face any discrimination for being a Sikh. Most of the time people are not even looking at you, they are only listening to what you have to say...'

Then there was the legendary Didar Singh Bains, who came to the United States in 1958, worked as a farm labourer and ended up owning over 12,000 acres of farmland in the United States and Canada. To date he gets his land blessed by the gurdwara priest and says, 'God owns it, I only work on it.' Says one of his neighbours, 'He grabs a handful of soil, sniffs it and can tell exactly what he can grow in it.'

One thing, however, that worries all Sikh NRIs is the future of their children: Will they be able to maintain their Khalsa identity? I have tried to address the issue in this book to the best of my ability.

As a bilingual counsellor at the Center for Multicultural Human Services (CMHS) in Falls Church, I worked with hundreds of families of South Asian descent. It warmed my heart to discover that not a single Sikh family availed of Public Assistance. Sikhs did, however, seek help and guidance to find their way around in the United States.

I had hardly completed the first round of interviews in my hometown, when I discovered that I was suffering from breast cancer. Fear, anger, depression and defeat succeeded each other before I was able to resign myself to the inevitable. The most difficult part was to accept the fact that I would never again see the two people who mattered the most in my life—my daughter Ranju and Sardar Khushwant Singh—who gave me courage to fight the disease. Life became a series of painful surgeries and therapies. During such difficult times, what sustained me was my implicit faith in my Gurus. Eventually I triumphed over cancer and was able to return to office and resume research for this book.

The stories in this book are of people who carved success for themselves out of alien surroundings. Their profiles may read like fiction at times but they are real people, no different than you and I.

I want to express my gratitude to my granddaughter Tarranum who typed the manuscript. Her sister Sitara occasionally lent a helping hand. I am equally grateful to my daughter Ranju and her husband Bryjinder Singh Kohli who stood by me during my illness and helped me to draw up my travel plans. I also wish to thank my brother Harjit who lives in New Jersey. He encouraged me to take time off from my regular job and do something that I could look back upon with a sense of satisfaction in the later years of my life. I am particularly grateful to my boss Dr Dennis Hunt, Executive Director of the Center for Multicultural Human Services, for allowing me to take time off from work to pursue my dream.

I would like to thank Roli Books, my publishers, for making it possible for me to take this research on diaspora Sikhs to a larger public.

Last, but not the least, I owe this work to Sardar Khushwant Singh, my mentor. He goaded me on to complete the book and provided the necessary support and guidance till I was through.

—Dr Surjit Kaur

UNITED STATES OF AMERICA

Introducing Sikhism to America

SRI SINGH SAHIB HAR BHAJAN SINGH YOGI

Bhajan Singh Yogi is a household name amongst the Sikhs of the Western Hemisphere although its very mention evokes a mixed response in Sikh circles. I had met him with Sardar Khushwant Singh in 1988 when the latter was updating his *History of the Sikhs* at the Wilson Center in Washington DC And then I met Yogi Bhajan in Chicago at the Parliament of World's Religion in August, 1933. I met him yet again at New York at a reception held by Shamsher Singh at the Shri Hemkunt Foundation. Each time I saw him I was impressed with the impact he had on the audience. He wore specially designed white gowns, huge diamond rings and necklaces. I wondered what yoga had to do with the millions of dollars worth of jewellery, or the number of disciples who accompanied him each time he attended an important meeting or a conference.

It was in 1998 that Sardar Onkar Singh, the elder brother of Sri Singh Sahib Jathedar Manjit Singh, invited me to present a paper at a seminar held in Phoenix, Arizona, in late 1999 to celebrate the tricentenary of the birth of the Khalsa. Jathedar Manjit Singh had been invited to be the keynote speaker at the seminar.

The paper entitled 'Status and Role of Women in Sikhism,' threw up some disturbing statistics: the declining ratio of females as compared to males in Punjab. The chairperson grew impatient and told me to wind up. Yogi Bhajan who was sitting in the audience yelled at the chairperson. 'The speaker is just beginning to make her point,' he turned towards me and said, 'Bibiji carry on with what you have to say.' His intervention notwithstanding, I decided to wind up my presentation without detailing the statistics.

I was to learn soon enough that Yogi Bhajan was in favour of women's liberation and disliked American expressions such as 'babes' or 'young chicks' for women. He proclaimed that he would transform these 'chicks' and 'babes' to 'hawks'.

Later on in the course of an informal meeting with Yogi Bhajan, where he was surrounded by his admirers including Jathedar Manjit Singh, he casually came out with his story: 'When I arrived in Los Angeles in 1969, the Indians including Sikhs refused to talk to me. They looked down on me as I had no qualifications to make good in this country. But today they sing a different song.'

Yogi Bhajan has travelled a lot, taught a lot, and accomplished something beyond anyone's imagination. And the satisfaction of having made a difference to so many lives simply compensates for his poor health today.

I undertook a journey to Española where Yogi Bhajan has lived for the past thirty years. When I arrived at the airport of Albuquerque, I was met by Sutanter Singh, a handsome young man with a turban and a long beard. He was nattily dressed in a Punjabi *kurta pajama*. Immediately putting me at ease, he took charge of my luggage. We arrived at Guru Ram Dass Place in Española. I was taken to a guest house, which was spotlessly clean and tastefully decorated with paintings and artifacts. It was lunchtime. We walked up to Yogi Bhajan's home where his wife, Bibi Inderjit Kaur, was waiting to receive us. She led us to a room where Yogi Bhajan was sitting in a revolving chair, watching TV in the company of his fellow Sikhs.

A bevy of American beauties all dressed in white, looking as sexy as fashion models arrived soon after. Since Yogi Bhajan's son is in the jewellery trade, some of these ladies had brought along samples of semi-precious stones to show to Yogi Bhajan. Yogi Bhajan watched an Indian movie on TV and listened to them and me, simultaneously. His diet of cucumbers seemed to be related to his poor health. Every now and then, he cracked a joke or made an observation which elicited a reaction of admiration from those around him. Occasionally two hefty men helped him to go to the bathroom.

One morning, as I sat with him and his wife, I saw an American Sikh, his personal secretary, combing his long hair.

Bibiji stays in her own premises and is in charge of the kitchen. She looks after the guests. She told me, 'Yogiji is surrounded by these people all the time and you will not find him alone to talk to you, so why don't you interview me instead?' The idea quite appealed to me, so we proceeded to her bedroom for an interview that I could record immediately and transcribe later.

Dr Inderjit Kaur is known as Bibiji amongst Yogi Bhajan's disciples. Keeping pace with her is difficult as she is so full of energy. At 3 a.m. she knocks on my door to wake me up. It's time to go to the gurdwara to listen to *Asa di war* sung by Bhai Avtar Singh.

Yogi Bhajan was born on 26 August 1929 in the village Kot Harkaran, Tehsil Wazirabad in the Gujranwala district, now in Pakistan. He grew up in a religious environment, with his grandfather, Bhai Fateh Singh, playing an important role in shaping his life. Sant Hazara Singh, a very powerful saintly figure, was instrumental in teaching him Kundalini as well as Tantrik Yoga.

He worked for the Government of India for over eighteen years as a Customs Officer, and taught what he had learnt from Sant Hazara Singh to his colleagues in Delhi and wherever else he was posted. Although he was well known as a yogi, he was deeply rooted in Sikhism. In 1960 he was posted in Amritsar. He and his wife, Bibi Inderjit Kaur rose early to wash the floors of the Golden Temple everyday for over four years. Through this act of faith, he forged a personal bond with the Guru—Guru Ram Dass—who first started to build the Temple. The Guru wrote: 'The Harmandir Sahib is the nucleus of a spiritually powerful centre, where the heavens and earth meet to bring harmony. It is not only in India, the Golden Temple is at two places—one is located in the heart of the seeker, the Sikh, and the other on earth in the city of Amritsar.' (Yogi Bhajan, Beads of Truth, 1971, cited in *History of Sikh Dharma of the Western Hemisphere*, 1995, p. 4, a Sikh Dharma Publication, Española, N.M., USA.)

When Yogi Bhajan decided to emigrate to the United States, people wondered how a man nearing his fiftieth year could give up his job for an unknown future? But Yogi Bhajan was only responding to an 'inner urge' to take the message of Guru Nanak to the West.

Yogi Bhajan arrived in Canada in 1968 only to find out at the airport that his entire luggage had been lost. The only belongings he was left with were the clothes on his back. To make good the loss, the airport authorities gave him a cheque which he tore up in front of them, declaring, 'I am not a beggar, I am a Sikh of my Guru, I don't accept alms...'

In the early '70s the Hippie movement had touched the lives of many people. Educated youth had rebelled against conventional society and materialistic, competitive values. They had set up cultural centres where they assembled, played music, consumed alcohol and drugs. One such centre heard about Yogi Bhajan, who was then in Canada, and invited him for a lecture. Soon after Yogi Bhajan received an invitation to speak before an audience in Los Angeles. On 5 January 1969 he delivered his first lecture to the American audience, and became an instant success.

Shakti Parwah Kaur, one of his earliest students, believes that Yogi Bhajan never judged anyone nor did he ever preach. 'He only talked to us about the way drugs affected our lives, then exposed us to an alternative way of life that brought out the best in us. He taught us to rise early, take a cold shower and do Kundalini Yoga. Kundalini Yoga makes you feel good immediately. It releases your dormant energies and you don't feel the need for drugs or alcohol.' She also said that Yogi Bhajan had never planned on converting anyone to Sikhism.

'It just happened. We were not looking for a new religion either. But one of our classmates decided to be like Yogi Bhajan, and look like him because Yogi Bhajan looked so handsome.

'The first American to wear a turban was Guru Singh. He is also the first American Sikh in the history of the Sikh Dharma. Others followed. They were mostly hippies who already had long hair and beards. All they needed to learn was how to tie a turban. Then they went to the local gurdwaras every week and found out where they could buy kurta pajamas. Yogi had always been partial to white, so his disciples decided to wear white,' observes Shakti Parwah Kaur.

Shakti Parwah Kaur has been with Yogi Bhajan since December 1968. She resents the word 'convert' and does not see herself as one.

'Yogi Bhajan never tried to convert anyone to Sikhism,' she insists. 'He was only trying to get these hippies off drugs and onto a spiritual path. And we are all so grateful to him for the new life he has given us. We couldn't have asked for more,' she says.

As the conversation progressed, Shakti Parwah Kaur felt more at ease to talk about herself and her deep affection for Yogi Bhajan.

'You know I was a young woman in my thirties, working as

a waitress in one of the posh restaurants in Hollywood and making enough money.' With her looks that was hardly difficult to believe.

Shakti Parwah Kaur was amongst the audience at the Cultural Center that invited him from Canada to speak to the youth—mainly hippies with long hair and flowing beards—seeking spiritual enlightenment.

'I really felt sorry for the yogi. He had no money, no friends and he did not ask for anything.' She started bringing lunch for Yogi Bhajan, who charged 75 cents per session for teaching yoga. She also helped him get a Green Card, then an American citizenship.

From the many stories that I had heard from his earliest disciples who now hold key positions in Yogi Bhajan's business and social organizations, it seems that the first two to three years were wrought with difficulties. During 1968–69, when Yogi Bhajan had just started teaching yoga at the East-West Center in Los Angeles, he received busloads of hippies keen to learn yoga from him. The director of the centre did not want the centre crawling with hippies, and Yogi did not want to abandon them. So he took up another place to conduct his yoga classes. Soon after one of the hippies' relatives who owned a furniture store gave him a room where he could conduct his classes.

Yogi Bhajan didn't make enough money to rent an apartment. He stayed either as a guest or a paying guest in other people's homes. Shakti Parwah Kaur told me that once, Yogi Bhajan was thrown out of a home because the owner complained that he got up too early. As though that were not enough, the owner's live-in girlfriend had started getting up early as well to do yoga!

Yogi Bhajan's popularity spread from California to the other states. In the late '60s and early '70s people were looking for answers to serious questions. Yogi Bhajan had something valuable to offer. Soon he acquired a large following in Los Angeles. Hollywood swore by him. Invitations poured in from other cities requesting him to set up his yoga ashrams there. He had to travel a lot and worked 18–20 hours a day. This was bound to take a toll on his health. He developed diabetes and heart problems, and had to undergo a triple bypass heart surgery. When he started teaching Kundalini Yoga, he had no idea that some day a large number of his disciples would become 'Khalsa Sikhs'.

In the *History of Sikh Dharma,* Yogi Bhajan's disciple Santi Kaur Khalsa wrote: 'When the Americans visited the Golden Temple at Amritsar, they touched the roots from where they had grown. For the first time the new Western Sikhs were bathed in the golden light reflecting from the walls of the Harmandir Sahib, absorbing them in the love of Guru Ram Dass. They realized that it was to Guru Ram Dass that they belonged. They had come home at last.'

Santi Kaur went on to describe the inspired moment when 'the universe lost a beat' as the new Khalsa of the West found themselves at the doorsteps of the Golden Temple.

'So moved were they by this first experience at the Harmandir Sahib that many of the young Sikhs asked to receive the sacred *amrit,* to be initiated into the fellowship of the Khalsa. They reverently prepared themselves and in the pre-dawn hours they walked with Yogiji around the marble *parikarma* to the door of the Akal Takht. Here he stopped and with a gentle hand on their shoulders he sent them upstairs alone, telling them, "I have brought you to the Guru's feet, and now my job is done. The rest of the distance you must walk alone."'

On 3 March 1971 at an impressive ceremony, the Jathedar of the Akal Takht presented Yogi Bhajan with a sword of honour and a *saropa*. The title of 'Sri Singh Sahib' was conferred upon him and he was presented with a letter of authority from the Shiromani Gurdwara Prabandhak Committee (SGPC) to establish a ministry for Sikh Dharma in the Western Hemisphere.

In keeping with the Sikh tradition as taught by Yogi Bhajan, these Sikhs rise early—at 3 a.m. to be precise—take a cold shower, do Kundalini Yoga, meditate and read the *Gurbani,* some in the English translation, and chant hymns from the *Guru Granth Sahib.*

Their favourite *shabad* is:

Gur sat gur ka jo sikh akhaye
So bhalke uth Hari naam dhiaavai
Uddam kare Bhalke Parbhatee
Ishnaan kare Amritsar naavai
Upades guru har har jap jaapai
Sabh kilavikh paap dokh leh jaavai
Phir charai divas gurbani gaavai
Behand yan uthdian harnam dhiaavi

[One who claims to be a Sikh of the Guru will rise and meditate on God's name. After making the diligent effort to rise early, he is then to bathe and cleanse himself in the Nectar Tank. Following the Guru's precept, he chants the name of God. By so doing, he will rid himself of all sins, misdeeds and bad Karma. Then he sings the Gurbani all day long, as sitting or standing he is in a prayerful mood. (Translation by Gurtej Singh Khalsa, Khalsa is Born in the West, *History of Sikh Dharma of the Western Hemisphere,* p. 8, a Sikh Dharma Publications, Española, N.M., USA.)]

There was considerable resistance from mainstream Americans to this newly adopted religion and lifestyle. Hundreds of young people who adopted the Khalsa tradition found themselves out of jobs. Having brought them to the Guru's door, Yogi Bhajan took it upon himself to steer them through their economic hardships.

Gurtej Singh Khalsa whose American name was Grey Harriman, became a Sikh at nineteen, while he was still in college and his parents were paying for his education. He studied English Literature and Philosophy, and with his high grade point average, was on the Dean's list.

His father ordered him to take off his white turban, shave off his beard or get out of the house. When he failed to comply he was thrown out of the house. Gurtej Singh decided to work his way through college by doing odd jobs, and then he got a fellowship. After graduating from college, he needed to look for a job. Gurtej Singh had learnt Martial Arts, and was interested in a career either in law enforcement or the military. His unconventional appearance, however, seemed to come in the way of landing such a job. When all doors seemed to shut, Yogi Bhajan instructed him to start his own business—guarding America's strategic places and people through Akal Security Inc.

Akal Security Inc., a security company was floated in Gurtej Singh's living room with the wise counsel of Dya Singh Khalsa, and the blessings of Yogi Bhajan. The corporation now employs 7000 Americans, ninety per cent of whom are non-Sikh Caucasian Americans. It provides security to federal buildings, federal courts, airports, industries, as well as security during social events, and sporting events such as football and basketball matches, to name just a few.

'How did you land your first contract and what was it about?' I asked Gurtej Singh, Founder President of Akal Security Inc.

'Our first federal contract was with the Department of Navy based in San Diego. We were to guard civilians. Our bid was competitive and we were very well clued up on the security business. Then on, there has been no turning back. We have established a solid reputation wherever we have worked,' said Gurtej Singh.

Gurtej Singh has been married twice. He has two children from his first marriage—a daughter and a son. The daughter died in an accident. The twenty-four-year-old son lives in New Delhi, India, manages Yogi Bhajan's house, and exports amongst other things, Indian furniture, artifacts, carpets, marble tiles. Gurtej Singh was divorced from his first wife in 1985 and met his present wife in 1989 when he went to Italy as the sole representative of the Sikh Dharma of the Western Hemisphere.

In the course of his two years in Italy, Gurtej Singh met the woman he was to marry in 1993.

'She is a medical doctor and had a hard time finding an internship in the United States. Then she ended up in Pittsburgh in a medical college that specializes in working with ethnic patients and foreign-born doctors. Now she has a lucrative practice in Española.'

During my stay in Española, I interviewed over a dozen American Sikhs and visited several offices. Each time I saw prominently displayed pictures of Guru Ram Dass and the Golden Temple. I remember meeting Dev Saroop Kaur, the Chief Executive Officer of Akal Security Inc., an elegant woman, who always kept Guru Tegh Bahadur's picture in front of her. 'Whenever I am perplexed or faced with a tough decision, I look at this picture and meditate . . . I let Guru Tegh Bahadur do my job whenever I am lacking,' she said with an intense look in her eyes.

At the moment there are fourteen different businesses being run by the Khalsa International Industries and Trades (KIIT). KIIT serves as an umbrella organization for an international group of varied companies.

In 1969 when Yogi Bhajan began teaching Kundalini Yoga in America, after every session he served a special spiced tea to his students which they affectionately christened 'Yogi Tea'. The same Yogi Tea was served in the Golden Temple restaurants that sprang up in Europe and in the United States in the early '70s. It is tasty, aromatic, and has medicinal properties. Yogi Tea is now reported to be the fastest growing tea company in the 12 billion-dollar natural foods industry. The organization runs over 5,000 natural food stores across America.

The actual chain of Golden Temple restaurants began in

1972 as Amrit Bakery in Springfield, Oregon. A year later Amrit Bakery moved its operations to Eugene, Oregon where for fifty dollars it bought supplies for Golden Granola. While Granola cereals have become very popular around the world, it is *Wha Guru Chew* that made history. *Wha Guru Chew* was developed late one night, while experimenting with leftovers from Golden Granola bars. By the '70s, *Wha Guru Chew* was in national distribution. In 1998 *Wha Guru Chew* celebrated its twenty-fifth birthday as the century's favourite healthy snack.

Yogi Bhajan seems to have developed a remedy for all ailments. He has also developed a line of almond oils called Sunshine Spa, specially meant for body massages. Yogi Bhajan may well have been one of the earliest entrepreneurs to use eastern technology and terminology to attract Westerners.

While Yogi Bhajan is reserved about his views on the political or religious leaders in Punjab, he is very vocal about the widespread use of narcotics and alcohol in the state. He is also very critical of the 'moral degradation of the people in Punjab'. Summing up his views on Khalistan in a single sentence, he said, 'We have to become Khalsa before we can demand Khalistan.'

I got a ringside view of Yogi Bhajan's birthday celebrations at El Dorado in Santa Fe in New Mexico. It was a grand affair to say the least. There were over 800 people from all over the country. Some political leaders from New Mexico were also present. Amongst them was the former Governor Bruce King who walked us through the history of Yogi Bhajan's achievements in America, fondly recalling the fledgling Sikh community he had visited during his first gubernatorial campaign way back in 1970.

'They were there in kind of makeshift tents trying to get started,' King said. 'I was nice to them and they were nice to me. But I figured they would be gone after a good wind or two came up.'

King, who ever since has received financial support from the

Sikhs for his campaigns said, 'They have never pressed me for anything but have taken a strong interest in children's issues.' King and his wife spoke highly of the American Sikhs' contributions to the community at large.

At the celebrations were the city's Who's Who, mostly Caucasian Americans and Yogi Bhajan's disciples from every corner of the country—all singing his praises. Congressmen came down from Washington DC. The Governor's wife wrote a poem in honour of Yogi Bhajan and said that the Sikh community in Española is a blessing and an asset to the nation. People danced on the stage. Some sang songs, others played their guitars. Yet others made speeches while many stood speechless. Yogi Bhajan arrived on stage in his wheelchair, then sat at the podium with two small children by his side.

Yogi Bhajan's elder son was out of the country selling Yogi Tea. Yogi Bhajan appeared to be in good spirits, but detached. He has already willed his lucrative businesses to the Sikh Dharma. That means none of his three children will inherit the assets that Yogi Bhajan has created in his lifetime. They shall eventually belong to the Sikh Dharma of American Sikhs.

Then his disciples whisked him away, even from Bibiji, his wife who has given him three children—Ranbir Singh, Kulbir Singh and Kanwaljit Kaur.

Shri Singh Sahib Har Bhajan Singh Yogi (Yogi Bhajan) seems to share a lighter moment with President Clinton during a special function organized at the former's residence.

Bibi Inderjit Kaur Khalsa with George Bush, the 41st President of the United States, and two followers of the Sikh Dharma of the Western Hemisphere.

UNITED STATES OF AMERICA

The Power Behind the Yogi

BIBIJI INDERJIT KAUR KHALSA

On 2 August 2001 Bibiji Inderjit Kaur was given a standing ovation for a host of reasons: her outstanding service to the community, her efforts in promoting the Guru's teachings amongst the American-born Sikhs, her contribution as Chairperson of the Clinical Therapists Committee of New Mexico and 3HO (Happy, Healthy and Holy Organization), her role as Ambassador to the United Nations NGOs (non-governmental organizations) and above all her generous hospitality at the Guru Ram Dass Place in Española, New Mexico.

I had met Bibiji briefly in the gurdwara in Washington DC and heard her talk in the United Nations about her activities at the 3HO Superhealth Organization founded by her husband Yogi Bhajan in 1969, and of which she is now the Executive Director. I had no idea of her background and what she had done to command so much respect.

When I went to Española to spend a few days at Yogi Bhajan's estate, I met Bibiji before I met Yogi Bhajan. She was down-to-earth, friendly, comfortable with herself and with everyone around her. She divided most of her time between the kitchen and her office next door where she kept two assistants busy. Her dining room which is connected to the kitchen through a window, is always packed with guests. And the home-cooked meals she serves are out of this world.

Late one afternoon I was summoned to her bedroom. It was a small room with white walls, white curtains, and bedspreads and cushions that were either hand embroidered or had crochet work. We took a few cushions each and made ourselves comfortable.

Bibi Inderjit Kaur was born on 21 January 1935 in the Gujranwala district, now in Pakistan. She studied in Khalsa School in Wazirabad until her family moved to Delhi after the Partition of India in 1947.

As a descendant of Bhai Abinasha Singh who treated Maharaja Ranjit Singh for small pox and who was given seven villages as a *jagir* in recognition of his services, Bibiji is indeed very proud of her ancestry.

In Delhi, she studied at the Sanatan Dharm College in Subzi Mandi. She was only seventeen when she was married to Bhajan, a distant cousin. He was a Puri, she an Uppal. After the marriage she came to live with her husband Harbhajan Singh Puri who was a customs officer at the Delhi airport. They lived in Nizamuddin and took a very active interest in Sikh affairs. Bhajan formed a Young Sikh Association and one of their activities was to organize *Shabad Kirtan* at his home in Nizamuddin once a month. He also taught yoga to his colleagues at the airport and to retired persons living in his neighbourhood.

In 1960 Bhajan was transferred to Amritsar. Bhajan and Bibiji decided to spend most of their spare time at the Golden Temple doing *sewa*. They spent a good part of their nights washing the floors of the parikarma and returned home at

3 a.m. only after the morning service had started. At 9 a.m. Bhajan left for office.

Four years later Bhajan was transferred back to Delhi. After spending two years in Delhi, Bhajan left for Canada from where he migrated to the United States in 1969. Bibiji stayed back in India with her three children.

In 1972 when Bhajan returned to India to take his wife and children back with him, 84 American Sikhs accompanied him on his visit.

Bibiji did not know where she fitted in either with the yoga ashram or with the hundreds of hippies who constantly surrounded Yogi Bhajan. Moreover he was away most of the time setting up the yoga ashram. So she decided to join her husband in his mission. She got up early to do yoga, meditate and read the *Japji Sahib* and the *Sukhmani Sahib* to the members of the ashram. She also cooked meals for hundreds of Yogi Bhajan's disciples. Besides cooking for them she cleaned their bedrooms, washed their clothes, and even taught the hippie women to dress properly in the ashram.

'They didn't bathe, they didn't wear underclothes, and they didn't wash their clothes,' says Bibiji looking back thirty years. Soon she started travelling to different ashrams.

Around the same time she also started cooking classes and taught Gurmukhi to disciples who were interested. She escorted *jathas* of American Sikhs for visits to the Golden Temple in India. There she introduced them to an old friend, Bibi Amarjit Kaur, who taught them how to do kirtan to the accompaniment of the harmonium and tabla. Later Bibi Amarjit Kaur too joined the mission in the United States.

Now people began to address Bibi Inderjit Kaur as Bibiji, and she became the mother of Yogi Bhajan's mission. Soon after she became the Bhai Sahiba or the Chief Religious Minister of the Sikh Dharma of the Western Hemisphere.

Bibiji was not even a college graduate when she married Yogi Bhajan. So she enrolled herself for three courses with her daughter Kanwaljit. Mother and daughter sat side by side in classrooms. Bibiji ended up with a string of A's. In 1981 she earned a Master's degree. This was followed by a Ph.D. in counselling in 1989. The Governor appointed her as the chairperson of the Clinical Therapist's Committee in New Mexico in 1991.

'Even my husband got his license for counselling under my signatures,' says Bibiji proudly.

Bibiji joined the Democratic Party. President Clinton appointed her Resource Woman for New Mexico. Since then she has been to the White House many a times.

In 1980 Yogi Bhajan developed heart problems and had to undergo an open-heart surgery with a triple bypass. This implied Bibiji taking over many of his responsibilities. She became the Executive Director of 3HO Superhealth Organization which was later affiliated with the United Nations.

As the Executive Director of 3HO Superhealth Organization, Bibiji has represented 3HO Superhealth Organization as an NGO at international conferences held in Egypt, China and Latin America. She has organized workshops on health and nutrition, and taught yoga and meditation, thus drawing worldwide attention to the 3HO Superhealth Organization's activities. In 1990 she was invited by the Soviet Institute of Sciences to establish programmes in health and nutrition in Moscow and other provinces of the former Soviet Union.

Bibiji served as the former President of the Indo-American Women's Association and is now a member of the World Affairs Counsel and the Los Angeles-Bombay Sister Society. In 1986 she and her husband established the International Peace Prayer Day observed annually in Española, New Mexico.

Bibiji has been recognized by her professional associates for her unique contributions in the field of counselling and therapy. In 1990, Governor King named her the Outstanding Woman in New Mexico, and in 1991 she was inducted into New Mexico's Hall of Fame. She also received recognition from the Governor of California for her work. Her name also figures on the international Who's Who of Intellectuals from Cambridge University.

Despite her public engagements Bibiji is a family oriented woman who values her children and grandchildren. She is happy that both her sons are involved with the activities of the Sikh Dharma of the Western Hemisphere. Her older son Ranbir Singh is the Vice President of fourteen businesses associated with the Sikh Dharma; her younger son Kulbir Singh is actively involved in building institutions in Punjab, especially the Miri Piri Academy in Amritsar, a school where American children study for their High School diplomas, but more importantly they learn Punjabi, Sikh history and philosophy, classical Indian music and the singing of the Gurbani. Her son-in-law Satpal Singh is also very supportive of the activities of the Sikh Dharma in the United States as well as in India.

Bibiji has been honoured at all the five Takhts of the Sikh Panth in India, with special recognition from the Jathedar of Takht Sri Kesgarh Sahib on the tricentenary of the birth of the Khalsa.

On 26 October 2001 Bibiji attended a briefing for leaders of non-governmental organizations in Washington DC. There she made it a point to apprise General Colin Powell, the Secretary for State who is deeply concerned about human rights issues, of the plight of the Sikhs in the United States and the hate crimes that have been taking place against them since 11 September 2001.

Bibiji and Yogi Bhajan spend half their time in India. They have built a huge complex called Institute of Psychological Studies through Yoga and Meditation, in Anandpur Sahib. Yogi Bhajan teaches this course once a year to the selected participants. It has some rooms for residential purposes too.

They have also built a school in Amritsar, and own a home in New Delhi.

UNITED STATES OF AMERICA

America's Richest Sikh

DIDAR SINGH BAINS

America's richest Sikh made his fortune growing peaches in California. At one time he was an ardent supporter of Khalistan. Today, Didar Singh Bains is passionately committed to a unified India.

I met Didar Singh Bains in the late 1980s. He was a tall, well-set man with a long beard, and acknowledged as the richest Sikh in America. He had bought a large building at the Capitol Hill, near the Library of Congress in Washington DC. Somehow after that I lost track of Didar Singh. One fine day I read about him receiving the Nishan-e-Khalsa at the Anandpur Sahib. On his return I called him up to congratulate him. He was as friendly and informal as ever, and said that he would be happy to see me in Yuba City, but warned me about his hectic schedule during the harvest season.

'Just give me a call from San Francisco as soon as you reach there, then we'll fix a date for you to visit Yuba City,' he said. Taking him for his word, I did exactly that.

It was with some difficulty, though, that my friend Gurbax

finally got through to him over the phone. I gave him a piece of my mind. He apologized and explained that every minute of his time meant money and that he was hardly getting any sleep at night.

'Harvest season comes once a year and this is how it is,' he said.

We fixed a time and place to meet. It was at a funeral home where the entire Sikh community was expected to assemble to bid farewell to a Sikh gentleman who had died of old age. Didar Singh stood at the head of the casket like a patriarch, receiving visitors and exchanging greetings. From there we drove across to his estate. We drove for miles through his orchards. He also took us to a tomato-canning factory on his estate. Conveyor belts transported hundreds of tons of tomatoes into cans. Once we were back in Yuba City, he took us to an Indian restaurant. Didar Singh looked tired. His beard had turned grey and he had lost weight. His eyes had lost their gleam.

'I had to undergo a heart surgery. They flew me in a helicopter to the hospital. That was three years ago and I have not been the same person again. I get very tired very soon,' he explained.

As we came out of the restaurant after dinner, we drove to Didar Singh's home. We were met at the door by Didar Singh's younger daughter-in-law wearing shorts and a sleeveless blouse. She is a pretty Punjabi girl with a very British accent. She led us to their luxuriously furnished living room. He showed us the bedroom Gurbax and I were to share that night and then led us to his office. I brought out my tape recorder and the list of questions that I had prepared.

Didar Singh has the memory of an elephant.

Born and brought up in the village Nangal Khurd, in the Hoshiarpur district, Didar Singh Bains was the third child of his parents, Sardar Gurpal Singh and Bibi Amar Kaur. Didar Singh's father came to the United States in 1948 and settled in Yuba City as a farm labourer. Didar Singh who was only ten years old at that time was left behind in the village along with his two elder brothers and four younger sisters.

'Our father used to send us money from the United States. With that we bought more land and our status in our village improved dramatically,' said Didar Singh with a sense of pride. As a teenaged boy Didar Singh studied in the local Khalsa School, and was in the school football team which was also the finest in Punjab.

'I too dreamt of going to the United States and working hard to make a lot of money, buy a lot of land and cultivate it with modern machinery. I wanted to own tractors, tubewells and pick-up trucks.'

Didar Singh was the first amongst his brothers and sisters to join his father in the United States in 1958. Life was hardly a bed of roses. Didar Singh stayed in labour camps and worked for 75 cents an hour, 18 hours a day sometimes. There were over 50 labourers in each camp who crammed into only four or five cabins for some sleep. He stayed in the camp for two years. Then he was promoted to the position of foreman, and given a jeep and a pick-up truck in which to drive around.

In four years he saved enough money and with a little help from his father, he set out to fulfil his childhood dream. He was only twenty-four when he bought 25 acres of land. Soon he moved into the largest farm in the State and became its richest Indian farmer.

A year later Didar Singh was introduced to a young lady, a college graduate and the daughter of a Sikh father and a French mother. He name was Santi Punian. Didar Singh was a shy young Sikh. After taking a year to make up his mind, he married Santi in 1964.

'Santi is a very intelligent and hardworking woman. You will meet her tonight.'

It was past 9 p.m. and Santi was still working at the farm where she was overseeing more than a thousand workers.

Two years after the marriage, the couple decided to lease 200 acres of Santi's father's farmland on which they grew apples, peaches and prunes. Whatever they saved, they invested in buying more land.

'When did your fortune really blossom?' I asked.

'In 1972,' he replied, after he ventured into a more profitable business—real estate. He decided to buy properties in cities where development was taking place, eventually pushing up real estate prices because of higher demand for housing. While he was talking to us about his real estate deals, his wife Santi walked in. He introduced us.

She had been working since morning and looked like an army officer in uniform. I apologized for inconveniencing the family during the harvest season and asked her to spare a little time for me. She begged to be excused saying she had been up since 5 a.m. and was very tired. Didar Singh came to her rescue.

'Santi has taken charge of finances. My daughter Diljit is back in Yuba City to help her mother.'

He pulled out a framed picture of Diljit from his desk drawer. I looked at it and exclaimed, 'Oh she is gorgeous!'

'That is the problem, she knows it too! She wanted to go into modelling, but I held her back. She can read and write Gurmukhi, do kirtan. She knows how to play the harmonium, and is a really caring person. She is so good with children and really cares about the poor, the needy, especially about the elderly. She is thirty-one years old and single. I tried to introduce her to young Sikhs but nothing has materialized so far. I worry about her future. She is such a talented and well-educated girl, and she is beautiful.'

Didar Singh continued, 'When I arrived here in 1958, I was a lad of twenty and there were no bearded Sikhs around. I too cut off my long hair and shaved off my beard. But I always felt guilty about doing that. In 1980 when the Jathedar of the Akal Takht visited Yuba City, I was re-baptized and became a Khalsa Sikh again.'

In 1968 Didar Singh was elected President of the gurdwara

in Stockton. In 1969 he began to build the first gurdwara in Yuba City. The local population of mainstream Americans were a little perturbed.

'We were not scared, we carried on with our plans. Now everybody is happy that we have our own gurdwara in Yuba City. There are about 10,000 Sikhs living in Yuba City,' said Didar Singh.

'Every year on the first Sunday of November they celebrate the Gurgaddi Diwas, widely known as the Day of the Sikhs. About 60,000 people gather in Yuba City that day. They come from as far as Vancouver, BC Canada; Seattle, Washington; Reno, Nevada; and other cities on the West Coast. People bring large quantities of food and hold individual *langars.* They put up earthen hearths to prepare *chhole bhature* and *mathian.* They also bring dry fruit, soda pops and snacks for children. We have so much food left over from this event that we donate large quantities to other charitable organizations like the Red Cross and the Salvation Army. We also collect donations and raise funds to the tune of over $100,000 for charitable purposes. They do the *Nagar Kirtan*, take out processions, full of colourful floats depicting Punjabi life in the countryside. The event is widely covered by the media—radio, television and the local newspapers.'

Didar Singh does not talk about his contribution to Sikh causes, but his friends and family say that he contributes upto $500,000 a year to Sikh causes, and is helping build a Sikh museum in Punjab. In 1998 he helped his daughter Diljit open the first Sikh preschool in Yuba City. The school now has a considerable number of students and Diljit plans to hand it over to the local Sikh youth to run it.

Friends and family in California say that Didar Singh is a one-man immigration machine. He has sponsored over 500 Sikh immigrations including those of his relatives. Many of them work in his orchards. Didar Singh is also known to have helped dozens of Sikh farmers in Yuba City start their own businesses by co-signing loans. In Canada, Didar Singh is financing a Punjabi school where thousands of Sikh children learn Punjabi.

'My dad has put in over one million dollars in that school,' Diljit told me over the phone.

Although a Republican himself, he donates generously to candidates from both parties. He is known to have given money to candidates from diverse political backgrounds—Gerry Brown, Pete Wilson, Vic Fazio, Walley Herger, George Bush and Al Gore.

In 1996 he brought Newt Gingrich to Yuba City and to his home by raising $100,000 for Gingrich's election funds.

After the 1984 riots when Sikhs were fleeing India, Didar Singh stepped in to find jobs for them in the United States. His attorneys were stationed in the Bahamas to assist both militants and non-militants.

Didar Singh visited India and his native Punjab in 1999 for the first time since he had left for the United States in 1958. During that visit he received the Nishan-e-Khalsa along with many other distinguished Sikhs amidst a crowd of nearly 100,000 Sikhs gathered at the Anandpur Sahib—the birthplace of the Khalsa. At the Kiratpur Sahib he immersed his father's ashes in the river flowing by the holy site.

During this visit he also resumed contact with his native village, Nangal Khurd. Since then he has been visiting Punjab regularly. He is concerned about the future of his community.

'It is my sincere advice to Sikh youth to not depend on farm living,' he says. 'Parents should provide a very sound education for their children so that they can find employment in non-agricultural sectors. Landholdings have become so small that you cannot depend on land alone for a living,' he adds.

Another source of disappointment for Didar Singh is the lack of appreciation for Sikh heritage.

'I am not only disappointed with my family, but with most other Sikh families.

'Take my own brother—he and his wife are both

Amritdhari Sikhs but their children have cut their hair and don't know a thing about their religion. I see a new trend in Sikh youth. At weddings, they get drunk and do *bhangra* until way past midnight. They just want to have fun.'

Didar Singh's views on Khalistan have changed.

'In 1984 Sikhs were angry with the Government of India. Even I wanted Khalistan. We were not fighting for a separate state, but for our people back home. Some good people were there, but they got sidetracked. Now no one in Punjab is supporting Khalistan. I think more power should be granted to the State of Punjab.'

Didar Singh Bains and his family with Newt Gingrich in their living room after a fund-raising event.

The beautiful, stunning and very successful Diljit Kaur Bains has her roots in Yuba City.

UNITED STATES OF AMERICA

Rich Farmer's Rich Daughter

DILJIT KAUR BAINS

I have not met Diljit Kaur Bains. She is thirty-one and unmarried. I have only heard of her from her father, Didar Singh Bains, and the Indians (Sikhs) in and around Yuba City. They all admire her for her PR skills.

'Diljit,' they say, 'is very caring, easy to talk to and a joy to work for.'

There are over a thousand employees at Didar Singh Bains's estate and they all adore Diljit. One reason for her popularity could be that Diljit speaks to Punjabi workers in Punjabi, to Hispanics in Spanish, and to Anglophones in English.

Diljit was out of town when I visited Yuba City to interview Didar Singh Bains. So I spoke to her over the phone a few times from Washington DC. Diljit talks little about herself but at great length about her father Didar Singh Bains.

'He loves his people, he loves his religion, and he is a philanthropist. He is hard-working, but he doesn't spend on himself, he doesn't take great vacations.'

Diljit has a hard time separating herself from her father.

Everything she does is at his bidding. She has, however, defied him by pursuing a career as a fashion model, and a fashion designer. She did well, but her father recalled her to manage his estate. And here she is, happy being back home in her *pind* Yuba City.

Diljit is also bitten by wanderlust.

'My thinking is very Western, but my eastern grounding is what makes me whole as a person,' she says. She has earned two Master's degrees from the University of Southern California (USC): one in Land Development and the other in Business Management. Her father could not have found a better manager for his large estate. And she shares his interest in community welfare.

In 1998 she started a Sikh preschool.

'There are seventeen trustees who govern the affairs of this school and make all the decisions. And I am happy to teach Punjabi culture, language, and Sikh history. The children learn the five *pauris* of the *Japji Sahib*, and yoga. They learn why we prostrate ourselves before the *Guru Granth Sahib*. They are also taught the Gurmukhi alphabet.'

'Do you ever visit Punjab?' I asked her.

'I went back to Punjab last year, and I admire the architecture of our famous gurdwaras because architecture is one of the subjects I studied in college,' she said.

'Which gurdwara are you talking about? I was curious.

'Anandpur Sahib,' she said.

'We were talking about your preschool . . . How many children do you have?' I asked.

'Between 32 to 36 children who go through our courses. They are way ahead of other children when they join regular schools. They develop faith in God and in the Guru like nobody's business. The other night I was driving back from Los Angeles with my little niece. She also goes to the preschool. On the way we ran into a hailstorm and I couldn't even see my way. She asked me, "*Bua*, are you scared?" And my answer was, "Yes, baby, I am very scared." "Guruji will show us the way," said the little four-year-old and leaned back in her seat. This is the kind of faith my father taught me.

'But I want to share with you a very painful and tragic experience of my life,' continued Diljit.

'Go ahead, I am here to listen to you and share your pain,' I replied.

'Auntie, I had a terrible accident a few years ago. I had to undergo brain surgery because my head was bleeding profusely. After the surgery I was in solitary confinement because my white cell count went down considerably. I didn't know whether I was going to make it. There was panic, and at times a little fear in my mind, but deep down I had faith that the Great Guru was with me and that I would be fine. Love of Guru Nanak and faith in self—these are the two main things my father taught me in my childhood days, and they are the greatest gifts he could have given me. I enjoy the other gifts too. Expensive cars, clothes, jewellery and what have you, but they are nothing compared to what my father passed on to me in my childhood in terms of religious faith.'

Diljit continues to be generous in her praise of her father. 'My father has the Guru's blessing. The Guru gives him wisdom, the vision to look into the future, and my father ends up making the right investments. Can you imagine he bought over 6,000 acres near the airport? Now that is no longer just arable land but real estate!' she says.

Although she has come home to Yuba City to work with her parents, manage their estate, and give back to the community at least a part of what she thinks was given to her, Diljit often goes away.

'I am not a small-town girl,' she says, 'But my roots are in Yuba City. I feel safe here.'

Diljit does plan to get married and have children, but Mr Right has not shown up yet.

UNITED STATES OF AMERICA

Fame and Fortune through Fibre Optics

DR NARINDER SINGH KAPANY

I had heard about Dr Kapany long before I met him in Phoenix, Arizona at a seminar on Sikhism organized by Yogi Bhajan to celebrate the tricentenary of the birth of the Khalsa. Dr Kapany was not very communicative and took a back seat during the proceedings.

I knew that Dr Kapany had established a chair in Sikh Studies at the University of California, Santa Barbara, which was headed by Gurinder Singh Maan who had done pioneering work on Sikhism at Columbia University. But I still didn't know how important Dr Kapany was to the Sikh community until Sardar Khushwant Singh pointed out that his profile must be included in this book.

I drove to the Kapanys' residence about fifty miles outside of San Francisco. My hostess Gurbax Kaur Kahlon from San Francisco had accompanied me to the Kapanys' residence. We were met by Dr Kapany at the gate. Mrs Satinder Kapany was busy getting high tea ready for us. She welcomed us with open arms and her charming smile, and proceeded to offer us Indian

Dr Narinder Singh Kapany mulling over his next project in Fibre Optics.

The erstwhile First Lady, Hillary Clinton flanked by Mrs Satinder K. Kapany and Dr Narinder Singh Kapany.

(Punjabi) tea, samosas and sweets. She apologized for her husband's 'unfriendly' response over the phone. 'Surjit, you are only trying to do your job, but my husband is getting funny ideas.'

That may well have been the case as Dr Kapany did not know me and I had kept calling up requesting an appointment for an interview!

Dr Kapany took us around to show the rare pieces of paintings and sculptures of distinguished artists including Sobha Singh and Arpana Caur. He also has a rare painting of Maharani Jindan done by an English painter.

Dr Kapany sat on a rocking chair. I made myself comfortable on the carpet, gave him the microphone of my small tape recorder and inquired about his past.

Narinder Singh Kapany was born on 31 October 1927 in Moga. He grew up in Dehra Dun and was educated in the famous Doon School and the local DAV college. His father Sardar Sunder Singh had taken early retirement from the Army and settled in Dehra Dun as an independent contractor.

Narinder Singh Kapany had a happy childhood in the secure lap of his mother, Bibi Kundan Kaur, and in the company of his many brothers and sisters. He still remembers how excited he was to receive a camera for his birthday from his father.

'I took many beautiful pictures with that camera, and that is how I got interested in fibre optics,' he says.

Narinder Singh Kapany graduated from Agra University in 1949 with Physics, Chemistry and Mathematics, then took up a job at the ordnance factory in Dehra Dun as a supervisor in optical instrumentation. In 1951, he left for the United Kingdom to join the Imperial College of Science and Technology in London, from where he received his Ph.D. in Technical Optics. Then began the era of fibre optics with over 100 patented inventions to his name: fibre optics, communications, lasers, biomedical instrumentation, solar energy, to name just a few.

I asked Dr Kapany if he had considered returning to India after getting his Ph.D.

'Yes, in fact I tried to go back after getting my Ph.D. from King's College in London. V.K. Krishna Menon, the then High Commissioner of India in the United Kingdom had become a friend of mine, and arranged for me to meet India's Prime Minister, Mr Jawaharlal Nehru in Delhi. I spent two hours with Pandit Nehru. He sent a note to the Public Service Commission about me. They were going to hire me as the Head of Defence Science Organization, but a year went by and I received no communication from India. So I decided to come to the United States in 1955. They did write, though only after I had already made my decision. Their loss!' We both laughed.

'When I came to the United States in 1955, there were very few Sikhs in this area. I was perhaps the only one for a while. But I was neither discriminated against nor persecuted for being a Sikh, and that is God's truth. Maybe that is because I only dealt with high-level officials. I started a company in the early 1960s and made it public in 1966. Don't let anybody tell you that being a Sikh is a disadvantage. You have to have the courage of your convictions. There are a lot of Sikhs who have given up being Khalsas. It is ridiculous. A Sikh's appearance is a mark of distinction.'

Dr Kapany started his career in 1952 and is still working in the same field. Not only is he a patented inventor, but also the author of 4 books and over 80 scientific papers. After holding a managerial position at the Illinois Institute of Technology and Research, he became the President and Director of Research at Optics Technology Inc. in Palo Alto, California. From there he went on to become the Chief Executive of Keptron Inc. before starting K2 Optronics in Palo Alto, in 1960.

He made a fortune through his scientific innovations that benefited the fields of communication and medical technology. His success in these fields opened up other avenues for him to explore his talents. He was noticed by the academia, and invited by the University of California Berkeley and Santa Cruz to teach and guide post-graduate students. Dr Kapany has also been the Director of the Center of Innovation and Entrepreneurial Development (CIED) at the University of California at Santa Cruz. He has done, and still keeps doing much for the advancement of research and technology in the field of fibre optics, and has been referred to as an unsung hero among five other selfless geniuses of the world.

Dr Kapany is passionate about art and literature. He started a philanthropic organization almost thirty years ago with a view to preserve Sikh heritage, and make sure that Sikh traditions are handed down to Sikhs living in Europe and North America. He says his aim in life is, 'to pass on Sikh heritage and traditions to the Sikh diaspora in the West particularly to the youth and to introduce the world to Sikh ethics, mysticism, arts, literature and heroism and advance Sikh culture.'

The Sikh Foundation has produced 25 books on Sikhism. There are four to five more projects in the offing. A Sikh Studies Center has already been established at the University of California, Santa Barbara, and four more centres are planned for various universities in California.

'Through these centres,' says Dr Kapany, 'More literature on Sikhism will be produced in the next ten years than what Sikhs have produced in India thus far.'

Dr Kapany has projects in India as well.

'We are trying to renovate the Guru ki Maseet in Hargobindpur in Punjab.'

'What is the Guru ki Maseet?' I asked.

'People don't understand what Sikh religion is all about. It is a very tolerant religion. No one knows that Guru Hargobind had built a mosque called Guru ki Maseet for the Muslims of his days.'

Dr Kapany organized the first international exhibition of Sikh artistic heritage to celebrate the tricentenary of the birth of the Khalsa. The exhibition gathered under one roof original Sikh art from international archives. It was opened on 25 March 1999 at the Victoria and Albert Museum in London, from where it travelled to the Asian Art Museum in San Francisco in 2000. Later it was taken to the Royal Ontario Museum in Toronto, Canada.

Dr Kapany gets up early in the morning and starts his day with prayers. He works in his office till late and takes a little exercise before dinner.

Khalistan appears to be a sore spot with Dr Kapany. He said, 'In 1984 a lot of people were killed. These killing were unrelated to Khalistan. It was a disaster. I gave several interviews on radio and television in which I thoroughly criticized the Government of India for what it did to Sikhs in India. The Khalistan movement did not produce what Sikhs really wanted. Khalistan is not the answer. Compared to 1984 and before, look at the number of Sikhs in India now. A large percentage of Sikhs in Punjab have cut off their hair. . . the number of Sikhs in Punjab has gone down considerably.'

Dr Kapany is disillusioned with the leaders of the community.

'They are the saddest part of India, our Sikh leaders in Punjab. They lack in ability and understanding of what needs to be done. Corruption is rampant. Religious leaders are no better. I cannot think of any Sikh leader who deserves my respect,' he says emphatically.

Dr Kapany's own children are both married to Caucasian Americans. He is only hoping that his grandchildren will opt for Sikhism as the religion to live by. At this point becomes pensive and says, 'But who knows?'

I had a few minutes with Mrs Kapany. She told me that she was studying English Literature in London when she met her future husband. They met each other many times before they got married in 1954 in the oldest gurdwara in England, in London's Shepherds Bush.

Dr and Mrs Kapany have two children. Their son, Raj Kapany is the Chief Executive Officer in Fiber Optronics. Their daughter Kirin is a lawyer, and married to a film director. They have similar professional interests and are happy together. Mrs Kapany adds, 'We searched high and low in our Sikh community and finally found someone who she grew very fond of, only to discover later that the man was already married. . . so what can you do? My daughter was disillusioned. Then she met this young white man. I think they are in love with each other.

'The good thing about our children and grandchildren is that they all go to gurdwaras.'

UNITED STATES OF AMERICA

Money and Culture

KAVELLE AND KULJIT BAJAJ

In October 1998 I received a dinner invitation from the Bajaj family living at Norton Road, in Potomac, Maryland. The Bajajs are perhaps the richest Indian family in the tristate area.

'What can I have in common with them?,' I asked myself. I was very reluctant to drive to Potomac in the dark to dine with people I had never met before. However, I did venture out. When I finally located the house, I was given a number for valet parking and then I went in. I saw many familiar faces there. This was such a pleasant gathering—a mixture of Sikhs, Hindus, Punjabis, Bengalis and a few Americans. I went looking for my hosts Kuljit (Ken) and Kavelle. Standing amongst the glamorously dressed ladies there she was, wearing a simple *salwar kameez,* and a *dupatta* thrown around her shoulders. She was welcoming the guests with her warm smile, and her husband Ken was serving drinks.

Over 400 people had been invited. Exquisite china, starched cloth napkins, and shining silverware were laid out on the table. No paper plates, no paper napkins, and no plastic spoons! At the end of the evening I went to Kavelle to thank her for including me in her guest list. She asked me about my work. Since then I have been to her lovely home every time there was kirtan or an *Akhand Paath.*

More recently I went to see the Bajajs to interview Kavelle for this book. We sat in her spacious lawn, then Kavelle took my friend and me around to show us her rose garden and the marble statues she had imported from Greece.

Her ageing mother, Mrs Agya Kaur who has lived with her off and on since 1978 joined us.

'Kavelle has had a very good education and she takes care of everyone,' she said.

We moved indoors to talk to Ken and Kavelle. Kavelle is the youngest of three children. She had seen her father in his heyday as well as when he suffered setbacks in his business. She was brought up in a traditional family environment where girls were allowed to get enough college education to fall back on, and taught to be a good wife and mother. She has a B.Sc. degree from Lady Irwin College, Delhi.

One day her parents saw an advertisement in the newspaper: 'A young Sikh, Ph.D. in Engineering, settled in America, looking for a suitable match...'

Kavelle was not keen on leaving India. She had heard stories about women having to work hard at home and outside. The first time she met Ken, she talked her head off and went home complaining about Ken being too quiet and reserved. Kavelle's father asked her to give Ken another chance. After that they met several times. Six months later she was completely smitten.

'I was in love with Ken before we got married,' she says with tears of joy in her big bright eyes.

'I came to live with my husband in his small apartment in Detroit City. We are blessed with two sons, Sunny and Reuben. My mother came from India to help me with the kids.'

When the boys grew up, Kavelle took up a job as an assistant to a dietician in a hospital. Her employers were happy with her work but she felt she could do better. She quit the job and joined college to take classes in Computer Science. Meanwhile, Ken urged her to do something on her own.

'In a few years your sons will go to college, I will have my profession. You too must have something to took forward to?' said Ken.

She had watched her husband grow in his profession. She saw how computer technology was rapidly changing the world, and felt her future lay in computers. In 1985 she started her own computer company, I-Net and became its Chief Executive. The company provided network services to a 1000 companies, and to the United States Government including NASA and the Department of Defence. In three years the company was recognized amongst the best in the region. At this time Ken joined the company. They made an unbeatable team. She focused on strategy and administration, he focused on marketing and operations.

Ken had worked for Electronics Data System (EDS). In 1979 he won a 656 million-dollar contract. He supervised the data management process for the same project until 1984 when the company was acquired by General Motors (GM).

In 1996 Kavelle decided to sell I-Net to pursue other interests. At that time she made another major decision that was to benefit the American community at large, including Hindus, Sikhs, Muslims and similar ethnic communities—to start the Bajaj Family Foundation, a charitable organization that would promote arts, especially Indian art and music, and help individuals who needed support to realize their talents. Today the foundation also helps non-profit organizations carry out community projects to promote literacy and self-sufficiency among the immigrant communities. For the tricentenary celebration of the birth of the Khalsa, she produced a CD *Sant Sipahi.* She also sang the Gurbani. Her organization prepares educational material 'on modern Western lines' for the new generation.

Kavelle and Kuljit Bajaj shortly after their wedding in New Delhi.

The perfect family—Kavelle and Kuljit with their sons Sunny and Reuben.

'Music and fine arts have a universal language, and appeal to the hearts of people, young and old, from all corners of the world,' says Kavelle. So she and her husband have decided to promote Indian art and music by sponsoring courses through the regular degree programme at George Mason University in Northern Virginia.

The plan will offer programmes in Indian classical and folk music and performing arts for students and the community. Kavelle feels that for ethnic communities to integrate into the American mainstream, there should be an understanding and an awareness of cultures. And music and arts are a great way of doing this.

In 1998 Ken and Kavelle started APPNET system. The company provides electronic commerce solutions. It went public in 1999 and was sold in June 2000 to Commerce One.

Kavelle is a deeply spiritual person and has a broad perspective on Sikh religion and Sikh values. She has the most beautiful room for the *Guru Granth Sahib* in the centre of their home and does *paath* and sings the Guru's hymns regularly. She says that whenever she is faced with a difficult decision, the Guru's *shabad vaak* guides her. She is a little concerned about her sons growing up in this country. 'They can get lost in this environment, other cultures dominate . . .' That is why the Bajaj Family Foundation is taking up projects to produce educational material on Sikh religion and cultures, so the future generations will know of their rich heritage.

It is quite a challenge to talk to Ken. He does not mince words and gets impatient with people asking personal questions. He went to college in Ludhiana and got his engineering degree from Guru Nanak Engineering College. Despite standing first in his college and fourth in the University, he could not find a job in India.

'I gave my country a chance to keep me, but . . .'

He left for Germany and worked there for nine months before coming to Canada. In Canada he obtained a Master's degree in Electrical Engineering from the University of Toronto, then moved to Detroit, Michigan, in the United States to earn a Ph.D. in Computer Science. In December 1973, he went back to India and got married to Kavelle.

'Do you ever look back?' I asked that question just to see his reaction.

'Look back? That was the best thing I ever did in my life.'

He also insists that Kavelle's and his was not an arranged marriage in the traditional sense, and that they were both free to make their decisions.

As things have turned out, they were fortunate to have met each other through the newspaper advertisement.

'I see that you have encouraged Kavelle to come to the forefront. Normally men from our part of the world like to keep their wives behind the scene,' I said to provoke a response.

He replied, 'My eldest brother had died in an accident at a very young age. As a child, I saw my brother's wife go through hardships that I would never want my wife to face, were anything to happen to me. I also believe all people are born equal, and every person, man or woman, has an equal right to develop his or her potential to the fullest. So I challenged my wife to make something of herself.'

Ken thinks that Kavelle is the most gifted and talented person he has ever met, and he feels proud to have been instrumental in the development of her career.

'We worked together and lived together for seven years until we sold our previous business. That is very rare in this country,' he observes.

Ken and Kavelle hold similar views on social issues such as the status of women, the dowry system, and women's education. They do not believe in giving large sums to gurdwaras as part of the *daswandh* but send fresh flowers to all the gurdwaras in the Metropolitan area. Ken is not religious in the traditional sense.

'I have cut my hair. I did not have to, there is no justification for it. I did it because I wanted to compete with Americans. Discrimination does exist, but it is hard to prove it.'

But Ken says his daily prayers, works 12–14 hours every day, gives to charity and tries to make a difference in the lives of all who need his help.

'Punjab should start an Internet university,' says Ken.

'And will you support it?' I ask him, as if to pin him down.

His response is most spontaneous, 'I'll be glad to invest in Punjab. I owe it to my people.'

He feels that Punjab has a lot to offer in terms of manpower to the rest of the world. Punjabis are the most forward-looking and hardworking people. And Kavelle shares his opinion: 'The greatest gift to me was my birth in a Sikh home. I have inherited the most modern religion in the world.'

UNITED STATES OF AMERICA

Tsar of Indian Hotels Abroad

SANT SINGH CHATWAL

The story of Sant Singh Chatwal's life reads like a chapter from a fairy tale. Having set out from a small town in Punjab, today he runs a worldwide chain of Bombay Palace restaurants. He aims to reach the elusive billion-dollar mark.

Sant Chatwal has been close to the Clinton family, and gave generously to Clinton's election fund.

'The Clintons discovered the flavour of Indian food through my restaurant in Washington and have become diehard fans,' says Chatwal. The Clintons love the Indian Pizza or naan, onion kulcha, fish malbar curry and *palak paneer.* But the former President's favourite is Indian kulfi.

Rumour has it that there were three C's behind President Clinton's visit to India in early 2000: Mrs Clinton, Chelsea, their daughter and Chatwal.

The earthquake in Gujarat in 2001, united the American Indian community throughout the United States, and the American India Foundation (AIF) was born. Sant Chatwal was very active from the New York area, and along with other community leaders persuaded the former President to make this trip to the earthquake affected areas. Clinton's visit to India from 30 March to 9 April 2001 along with a few American Indian leaders including Chatwal was a great success. It helped lay out a blueprint for rehabilitating the devastated villages. With the active participation of Sant Chatwal, two fund-raisers were organized in New York. These were well attended not only by the elite Indian Americans but by people from all walks of life.

A lot has been written about the terrorist strikes on the Twin Towers of the World Trade Center at New York on 11 September 2001. For the Indian American community, especially Sikhs and Muslims, the nightmare didn't end with the terrorist strikes. They had to deal with the backlash that left one person dead and many others bruised. News of hate crimes and racial slurs poured in from all parts of the United States. At this critical juncture, Sant Chatwal came to the rescue of the Indian community and of all those who felt persecuted, by approaching the New York Senators, Congressmen whom he knew, and even President G.W. Bush in Washington to save the bearded and turbaned Sikhs in the United States. The response was tremendous. Norman Minetta, Transportation Secretary, issued guidelines to the national airlines to respect the identity of all Sikhs. Colin Powell, Secretary of State, personally responded by sending a letter to Sant Chatwal hoping that the situation would normalize soon.

Some 2,000 Sikh Americans gathered for a candlelight vigil for the victims of the World Trade Center, at New York Central Park on 15 September. The entire Sikh community of New York and New Jersey, under the leadership of persons like Sant Chatwal, showed their unity and solidarity by making the event a great success.

Sant Chatwal was born in Rawalpindi, now in Pakistan, on 10 January 1946. His parents, Makhan Singh Chatwal and Sita Wanti, and their four sons and three daughters, moved to

Faridkot in eastern Punjab after the Partition of India in 1947. At the time Sant Chatwal was only one year old. After studying at Punjab University in Chandigarh, he joined the Indian Navy. He was also trained as a fighter pilot and was deputed on India's only aircraft carrier *Vitab.* He left the Indian Navy after a few years of service, as he did not see much of a future in the Defence Services.

In 1967 he went to Addis Ababa, Ethiopia, where he was promised a job in the airline of Emperor Haile Selassie. He turned down the offer after discovering that he was expected to doff his Sikh turban at the Emperor, cut his traditional long hair and shave off his beard. He found a job as a clerk that fetched him $300 a month, and helped a friend run a Lebanese restaurant. He saved enough money to buy the restaurant, and opened a second restaurant serving Indian food. Emperor Selassie officially inaugurated the restaurant.

In January 1971 Sant Chatwal was married to Daman Kaur in Mumbai.

By 1975 Emperor Selassie was overthrown. The new Marxist government took over Sant's assets and for the second time in his life, he had to think of starting afresh.

While in Ethiopia, Sant Chatwal had the better sense to take some of the proceeds from his restaurants, land investments and other ventures out of the country. Thus he had $400,000 in a New York bank.

From Addis Ababa, Sant Chatwal moved to London. Leaving his wife Daman and two young sons there, he toured North America to see where he could set up shop. After visiting a few cities, he landed in Montreal, Canada, which at the time still wore the Expo glow, and was looking forward to the 1976 Olympics. Sant Chatwal was charmed by Montreal and decided to settle there. After renting an apartment in Lachine, one of the first things he did was take a bus tour up to Westmount. There on Summit Circle was the house he decided he must have.

The house, Chatwal claims, belonged to one of Aristotle

Sant Singh Chatwal being honoured by the former Prime Minister of India, I.K. Gujral for becoming the Tsar of Indian hotels abroad.

Vikram Chatwal, Sant Singh Chatwal, Hillary Clinton, Bill Clinton, Daman Chatwal and Vivek Chatwal strike a pose for the shutterbug. The Clintons discovered the flavour of Indian food at a restaurant run by Sant Singh Chatwal in Washington.

Onassis's mistresses. That was not to deter him. Within a week of having 'chosen' the house, while his wife Daman and two young sons waited in the car, he knocked on its door and offered to buy the house which was valued at $160,000—at the time a third of all the money he had. Onassis's mistress was surprised, but sold the property all the same. The following week the family moved into the house, and the elder son Vikram was enrolled in Roslyn Elementary School. The rest of Sant's money went into the Bar Salon Les Copains on St. Denis Street, and his first ever Bombay Palace in Canada.

In Montreal, he came up with an incentive scheme for his executive chef and top managers.

'Even if I were to sit there 18 hours a day, it would still not be possible for me to be everywhere. I couldn't be in the dining room and the kitchen at the same time. The finest solution was to give them a slice of the pie, a part of the bottom line, so they would be looking to make more money for themselves, and naturally more for me. In the restaurant business you don't need the usual layers of executives. You need the right workers, who really produce the bottom line, not people sitting in head offices playing musical chairs,' says Chatwal.

In 1979 Chatwal used his profits from Montreal to open his first Bombay Palace in the United States at 75 Rockefeller Plaza, in Manhattan.

Chatwal chooses his sites shrewdly and drives a hard bargain on rents. In 1984, while looking for a restaurant space in Beverly Hills, he found a not very profitable French restaurant whose owner was paying $12 a square foot on the fashionable Wilshire Boulevard. By December 1986 Houston, Washington, DC, Chicago, Denver, San Francisco, Beverly Hills, Vancouver, Toronto, Montreal, London, Budapest, Hong Kong and Kuala Lumpur, all had their own Bombay Palace.

While Chatwal is more than happy to serve drinks to his customers, he and his wife Daman rarely drink and are fanatics about jogging and calisthenics. Daman Chatwal spends several hours a day at the Bombay Palace in Manhattan, supervising the staff. Chatwal has done a good bit of trading in Manhattan realty. In 1984 he bought a 10,000 square foot property at Second Avenue and 93rd Street, putting down $470,000 as deposit. Within six months he sold it at a profit of 4 million dollars. Today, Hampshire Hotels & Resorts control ten hotels in Manhattan, two in Canada and one barely minutes from London. The group is the single largest private hotel group in New York City.

Meditation and exercise, Chatwal says, give him energy for a 16-hour workday. A tall, lean man, Chatwal walks to work from his penthouse on the Upper Eastside, New York City. The walk gives him time to think, he says. What does he think about? 'Business mostly.' Asked about the secret of his success, Sant Chatwal simply says, 'Hard work, and a good dependable staff.'

Chatwal is serene and healthy-looking. Apart from jogging and a brisk walk through Central Park to work every morning, he finds spiritual regeneration in prayer and meditation.

'I meditate religiously every morning for 45 minutes. I read my holy book and pray. That really releases all the pressure and I feel grateful to God Almighty.'

He has encouraged his sons to do the same.

'I teach them the spiritual side of our culture,' he says. The importance of the values that are part of his oriental heritage cannot be underestimated. While the younger son Vivek looks after Finance in the corporate office of Hampshire Hotels & Resorts LLC, on Eleventh Avenue, Manhattan, the elder son Vikram is the person to watch.

By the time Vikram was at the prestigious Wharton School of Business at the University of Pennsylvania, the family was heavily into hotels. Not long after Vikram graduated in 1994, his father began looking to expand into the trendy boutique market. Vikram took charge of the new division.

Vikram Chatwal is a hotelier, model, dilettante film producer, and international entrepreneur rolled into one. He manages The Time, his New York boutique-hotel, that he opened two years ago to elbow his way into the lucrative market of fashion-conscious consumers willing to pay a premium for cool luxe. Set in New York's fabled Times Square, the building's transformation from a dive into a modernist boutique-hotel paralleled the gentrification of the intersection itself.

The concept has attracted an army of the urban hip, and notorious celebrities. Hillary Swank, Luke Perry and Mike Tyson have all stayed here. So have the bands Green Day and Blink 182. Visitors to The Time include Robert de Niro, Sean Combs aka P. Diddy, and Claudia Schiffer.

The boutique-hotel's popularity has made Vikram not a flunkey of the celebs, but a quasi-celebrity himself. He has featured in the *Vogue*, from the American to the Italian editions. Articles have been published about him in most languages, all over the world.

Vikram has only gone from strength to strength—from The Time in New York City to Bush Hall a historic country house-turned-hotel outside London, and back to Montreal. There, three years ago, he bought the exquisite beaux-arts style Chateau Versailles and set about renovating the building. He added a funky restaurant bar, La Maîtresse, in the hotel's modern annex that was designed by Michael Joannidis, a young Montrealer, who at thirty-two, was an Oscar co-winner for the lighting technology he had invented. If The Time boutique-hotel in New York City is young and hip, the Chateau is quite the opposite—stately with touches of Old-World luxury.

To round off his glam life, Vikram is even trying his hand at producing movies with business partner and pal, Gaurav Chopra, son of New Age Guru, Deepak Chopra.

Despite his busy business schedule Sant Chatwal finds time to work for the community. He is the first Indian Founder Director of Asian American Pacific Caucus in Washington DC. He has been President of the International Punjabi Society, which has its head office in New Delhi and branches all over the world. In 2000, the International Convention of the International Punjabi Society was held in New York, where the First Lady Hillary Clinton was the Chief Guest at the main event in the Sheraton Manhattan.

Sant Chatwal is also the Chairman of the Sri Hemkunt Foundation Inc. in New York. This foundation organizes debates and seminars around the world for Sikh children and youth to educate them on moral and spiritual values. He is ever ready to contribute for any good cause.

Sant Chatwal has contributed in the field of media as well. He is the co-publisher of News India Group in New York, which publishes two weekly English ethnic newspapers, *News India Times* and *Desi Talk.* Both the newspapers have a very wide circulation.

Ironically, Sant Chatwal does not own a restaurant or a hotel in India. However Vikram has plans to open boutique-hotels in Mumbai in the near future.

Yes, he is full of love for his motherland and says, 'I yearn to build a hotel one day near the Golden Temple, the eighth wonder of the world.'

Based on 'Sant Singh Chatwal: Tsar of Indian Hotels Abroad,' *by C.S. Puri.*

UNITED STATES OF AMERICA

Dentist and Scholar

DR I.J. SINGH

Dr I.J. Singh's story is best told by him.

'I will always remember 14 August 1960, the day I landed in Idlewild Airport, later named John F. Kennedy Airport after his assassination.

'I had just graduated from Government Dental College in Amritsar. The Murry & Lenie Guggenheim Foundation had announced a competition for fellowships to study Pediatric Dentistry for a year. The fellowships were to be awarded to Indians. I applied on 2 January 1960 and was interviewed in Hyderabad. Six months later I was on my way to New York.

'The cabbie from the airport told me he was a Jew. I knew about Christians but had never heard of Jews. He invited me to his home for a Sabbath dinner. I learnt about the extraordinary kindness of New Yorkers and the complex mosaic that is contemporary American Society.

'At the end of the fellowship, I decided to stay on for another two to three years and pursue a graduate degree. The fees at the University of Oregon was almost one tenth the fees at New

York University or Columbia University. So off to Portland, Oregon I went.

'I acquired a Ph.D. in Anatomy from the University of Oregon Medical School and a D.D.S. from Columbia University. I have been here for forty-two years. The professional pursuit was not always easy. I learnt to work at night and go through graduate school during the day. This is the way many Americans live and so did I. It was a job at minimum wage (at that time $1.25 an hour), and I processed 400 to 2000 rolls of film every night.

'I became a US citizen many years ago.

'In the early 1970s thousands upon thousands of women (and also many men) marched down Fifth Avenue in New York to demand gender equality. My wife and I were watching the parade from the sidelines. Leading the parade was Gloria Steinem. I was perhaps one of less than a dozen recognizable Sikhs to be found in New York at that time and the only Sikh at the parade. Suddenly, one of the leaders of the procession, a woman spotted me and yelled, "Come join us, your women need this more than we do." I agreed and marched alongside others. On the way, I tried to tell her that women in India had more rights under the law than did American women, and that there were more women physicians and politicians in India than in America.

'The year I came here, 1960, was an important reminder of the openness of American society. It marked the first television debates between presidential candidates Richard Nixon and John F. Kennedy. The questions were blunt, the answers as honest as politicians ever give, and the post mortem of the debates by journalists absolutely ruthless. I wondered if Indian society could ever be so open.

'My claim to fame from those years is the time when I joined a protest against George Wallace, the segregationist Governor of Alabama who was then a candidate for the Presidency.

'Most Americans were always, and are even now, only

Dr I.J. Singh is a dentist of reckoning, and a scholar of Sikhism.

Dr. I.J. Singh, the father playing with his little daughter.

minimally knowledgeable about Sikhs or Indians. Many people would accost me on the streets in my earlier days and, after inquiring where I was from, wonder if India had colleges or cars or where I had learnt English.

'I was born into a middle-class family in Gujranwala, now in Pakistan. My father topped from High School through his Bachelor's degree which he completed with honours in Physics. Since he was one of nine children, and opportunities were limited, he joined the Punjab Public Service.

'My father urged me to join Government Dental College. I remember the Partition of India. We escaped one week later, on 22 August 1947 with the help of a Muslim truck driver.

'Sikhs are not new to America. The first Sikhs arrived in this country over a hundred years ago. They were mostly farmers and labourers. Educated Sikhs started arriving here after the British left India. It was a time when opportunities in Great Britain were rapidly dwindling while the gates to America were thrown open through its many scholarships, and fellowship programmes. Those who arrived in the late 1950s and early 1960s were young single students scattered across many university campuses. When I came to America in 1960, there were probably no more than two or three recognizable Sikhs in New York. The nearest gurdwara was in California, 3,000 miles away.

'Oregon was even more isolated. But driving around Portland in the early 1960s, one day I read a sign board—Punjab Tavern. On entering the tavern I met a lady in her sixties behind the bar. She was overjoyed to see me. She told me that when she was a little girl, there were Sikhs in the area who used to frequent this tavern owned by her father. Then there were racial problems, and all the Sikhs had moved either to California or Canada.

'In Oregon it was not uncommon for people to see me a lone Sikh with a turban walking around, and their missionary zeal would be aroused. Here was a soul who needed to be redeemed.

They would often invite me to their churches or schools to speak on Sikhism or India. In the beginning this posed a problem. What I knew of Sikhism was what I had learnt primarily by living in Sikh society, and not in any systematic fashion. Of India and Indian history, I knew very little. To teach others, I had to first teach myself. So I slowly learnt of the Sikh ways and also of the lives of my Jewish and Christian neighbours. This taught me to discover and appreciate the philosophical depth and the beauty of the Sikh faith. Often I claim that I was born a Sikh but regard myself as a convert to Sikhism. Four years ago I became an *Amritdhari* Sikh. But it is a journey that is far from complete and I remain a seeker on an unending path.

'While a graduate student in Oregon, I met a fellow student who was working for a Master's degree in Experimental Psychology. Pauline and I married in 1968 and moved to New York a year later. A daughter Anna Piar, a name derived from those of the two grandmothers, was born six years later. She remains the source of much joy and an occasional heartache. Our marriage was dissolved when Anna Piar was not quite three. In the years that followed, someone suggested the name of a young Sikh woman working in Canada. I called her. We talked on the telephone several times. Finally one day she said that we seemed to be so compatible we ought to meet. I agreed. Then she asked: "Before we meet I want to know whether you are a modern Sikh?" I was taken aback but recovered quickly and replied, "Of course, I am modern. I know which fork to use with which dish at dinner and absolutely never walk out of my house without clothes on. I am not entirely primitive. What exactly do you wish to know?" We all know what she was really asking—was I a *Keshdhari* Sikh? I never thought that being Keshdhari had anything to do with being modern. The former is an article of faith for a Sikh, the latter, a state of mind. Needless to say we never met.

'Over the years I sponsored my two brothers, a sister and my parents for residency in the United States. Soon the whole family was in New York. In 1990 I married Neena who was visiting her sister in Seattle. Meanwhile, my professional life moved along steadily. After the Ph.D. I completed a two-year stint as a Special Research Fellow of the National Institute of Health, then joined New York University in the faculty of Anatomy, where I am now Professor and Coordinator of Anatomical Sciences. Academia lives by the principle of publish or perish and I, too, have lived by it. Over the years I have published and presented over 100 research papers and reports in professional journals and books. I have also trained several graduate students and directed their doctoral research. Within seven years of having started as a new assistant professor I became professor, the only Keshdhari Sikh at that rank in New York University. I also hold Adjunct Professorships at Columbia University and Cornell University Medical School, and have lectured at many medical and dental colleges across the country. As a result of all my work, I have had a fair share of professional affiliations and recognition.

'Soon it will be time for me to retire. Has there been discrimination in my professional life? I would say yes but minimally. Yes, there is a glass ceiling but it is possible to push against it. I would not be quite so optimistic in any other society including the land of my birth, India.

'The most traumatic period for me as a Sikh was in June 1984 when the Indian Army stormed the Golden Temple. For several years after that the policies of the Indian government were designed and used to single out Sikhs for discrimination, arrests, even torture and killings. For many Sikhs, including myself this entire period has been one of rethinking the Sikh identity.

'India claimed that Sikhs were hell-bent on fragmenting the country by creating Khalistan. I believe that the successive Indian governments, and their short-sighted politics, have anyway brought the country on the brink of fragmentation. In principle I am not in favour of a religion-based identity for a state because in such a state there will always be a minority constituted of second-class citizens. Today can Sikhs uphold the idea of a separate state given that they themselves exist as a minority, no matter where they live outside Punjab?

'Slowly with my parents' help I started to build a respectable library on Sikhism and comparative religions. I started to review books on Sikhism. I must credit Professor N. Gerald Barrier for spurring me on in this direction. I wrote a few essays meant to chronicle my own progress on the path of Sikhism. Thanks to Professor Barrier, this culminated in a book of essays.

'It appears that as I am slowly winding up my career in teaching and research, I am developing a new interest which is equally gratifying. I cannot possibly describe the pleasure of examining and honing the many facets of our Sikh existence in the diaspora.

'When I look at how our Sikh community has grown in North America, and at the more than 100 gurdwaras that we have founded, I am elated. I have, however, some misgivings. We seem to be transplanting Punjabi gurdwaras into North American soil without heeding our needs here. There seems to be an unfiltered transfer of Punjabi culture, values and management models that do not meet the needs of the Sikh diaspora. Sikh leaders in Punjab and abroad seem oblivious of the needs of the diaspora.

'We often pay lip service to our *Rehat Maryada* but give no serious thought to it. Clearly it represents the will of the Sikhs and should be followed. But there is no reason why a conclave of the *Sarbat Khalsa* should not be convened to deliberate on it. There are many issues such as the place of women in our society, and our relationship with our non-Sikh neighbours that need to be debated and resolved. Female feticide is still practised in Punjab, and by Sikhs. Newer technology has thrown up fresh issues in bioethics. Dowry is yet to become a thing of the past.

'Since 11 September 2001, the situation has become very disconcerting. For many Americans a man in a turban looks too much like Osama bin Laden. Sikhs have been harassed at airports and in the streets. A man claiming to be a patriot killed a Sikh in Arizona. But President Bush, Attorney General Ashcroft, the FBI Director and many other high-ranking government officials have condemned the profiling and baiting of Sikhs. Such behaviour is uniformly described as un-American and contrary to American values.

'As tense as things can get on the street sometimes, America still remains the most open and tolerant society anywhere. Just a few days ago I met a man on the street. He appeared to be educated and his suit was definitely more expensive than mine. After chatting for a while he turned serious and somewhat apologetically asked, "Tell me, when your people came here why didn't they leave their religion back home?" I was flabbergasted for a moment. Then I finally turning to him, said: "Yes, I can answer that very briefly. Tell me, when your people came here why didn't they leave their religion back home?" For a moment he was nonplussed, but then he smiled. "You have a point," he said and walked away.

'When I talk to young Sikhs, my message to them, that I have distilled from my lifetime here, is just as it is possible to be a good Jew and a good American, or a good Christian of any sort and a good American, it is possible to be a good Sikh and a good American. The two terms are not mutually exclusive.'

Inherited Scholarship

DR NIKKY-GUNINDER KAUR SINGH

Dr Nikky-Guninder Kaur Singh was born in Ferozepur, Punjab. She grew up in Patiala. Her father was the renowned Professor Harbans Singh. Her home was the rendezvous of many a scholar. Her parents spent a year at Harvard University at the Center for World Religions. Her father held the first chair of the first department of Religious Studies at the Punjabi University. Nikky went to the Lady Fatima Convent School in Patiala but at home Sikh prayers and rituals were all-pervasive.

In 1972 Nikky joined Stuart Mall, Virginia a girls' preparatory school to finish her High School education. She was the first non-American in the school. When the local newspaper reporter interviewed her during her first week in the United States, he wrote: 'It seems as if Nikky Singh has lived in Virginia all her life.' At that moment, she told the reporter that she aspired to get a Ph.D. in the field of Comparative Religions and become a Professor. She obtained the highest GPA, and received the Daughters of the American Revolution Award for distinction in US History.

Nikky-Guninder Kaur Singh—brilliance epitomized.

Nikky-Guninder Kaur Singh with the writer Michael Ondaatje at the Sewa Awards in Toronto, Canada.

From Stuart Hall, Nikky went to Wellesley College where she majored in Religious Studies and Philosophy. She presented international news on her college radio station, and distinguished herself in academics. During her sophomore year at Wellesley she won the Meiling Soong Award for Best Paper. She graduated with the highest honours, including the Phi Beta Kappa and Durant Scholar. In her senior year, she did an honours project on the Physics and Metaphysics of the *Guru Granth Sahib*, which was published by Sterling in New Delhi in 1981. Her book received excellent reviews, and was launched by Gyani Zail Singh, the then President of India, at the Rashtrapati Bhawan.

Nikky began her graduate school in Religion at the University of Pennsylvania where she received the Dean's Fellowship. After her Master's degree she got her Ph.D. from Temple University in Religious Studies. She has been teaching at Colby College since 1986.

Nikky has published several books, including *The Name of My Beloved: Verses of the Sikh Gurus* (Translations from Sikh Sacred Literature), published by Penguin in 2001.

Nikky is regarded as one of the leading experts in Sikhism, and has lectured widely in the West including at Oxford, the School of Oriental and African Studies (London), University College, Cork (Ireland) and at several Canadian and American Universities.

UNITED STATES OF AMERICA

Life Dedicated to Science and Sikhism

BHAI HARBANS LAL

Dr Harbans Lal is Professor Emeritus and Chairman, Department of Pharmacology, the University of North Texas Health Science Center, and Professor Emeritus of Religious Studies, Guru Nanak Dev University in India.

Harbans Lal was born in Haripur, in the Hazara district of North Western Frontier Province (NWFP) in Pakistan on 8 January 1931. His father Beli Ram, was a practising physician and Mayor of the town. His mother was from the family of Dr Gopal Singh Dardi, the first person to translate the *Guru Granth Sahib* into English.

After taking the matriculation exams, Harbans left the North West Frontier Province for Uttar Pradesh in India with his mother and two younger siblings. He was the first student to be admitted to the newly founded Gandhi Memorial National College in Ambala for an F.Sc. degree in 1947. He then enrolled himself at Glancy Medical College of Amritsar in India for a B.Pharm. in 1949. After completing his undergraduate training in Pharmacy, he worked as a medical representative with Parke-

Bhai Harbans Lal (left) in his study surrounded by an equal number of books on Science and Sikhism (bottom).

Davis and Hoffman-La Roche initially in Bombay, then in Delhi before leaving for the United States in 1956 for graduate studies.

In the United States Harbans Lal completed a Master's degree in Pharmacology and Toxicology in 1958 from the University of Kansas, and a Ph.D. degree in Pharmacology from the University of Chicago in 1962. In 1961, he joined as Head of Department of the newly created Division of Pharmacological Research at the IIT Research Institute at Chicago.

He moved to the University of Kansas as Associate Professor of Pharmacology and Toxicology in 1965, and then to the University of Rhode Island in 1967 where he was promoted to the academic rank of Full Professor in 1970, only eight years after completing his Ph.D. He was invited to Janssen Pharmaceutica in Beerse, Belgium, to set up research groups on Behavioural Pharmacology and Toxicology.

In academic circles, Dr Harbans Lal is known for his research in the areas of Behavioural Medicine, Substance Abuse, and on the prolongation of a healthy lifespan.

He served on many national and international science advisory boards including National Institutes of Health and served for 14 years as the Editor of a monthly journal, *Drug Development Research.*

During his academic career, he published over 400 research papers, 20 books, several research reviews and 56 chapters in technical books, and was invited several hundred times to talk on his research, all over the world. The University of North Texas Health Science Center established a pre-doctoral fellowship award in his name in recognition of his work. Dr Harbans Lal supervised 32 doctoral students, and a dozen post-doctoral trainees. The Society for Neuroscience: Chapter of Scientists of Indian Origin crowned his efforts with the Award of Outstanding Senior Neuroscientist.

Being a *Sahjdhari* Sikh, Dr Harbans is known a Bhai

Harbans Lal. He began his Sikh activism during his schooldays, and went on to become President of the All India Sikh Students' Federation in 1954. In 1956 he left India for the United States to pursue higher education.

In 1995, Guru Nanak Dev University awarded him the degree of Doctor in Literature, honoris causa, in recognition of his contributions to Sikh Studies. On 14 April 1999, the Anandpur Sahib Foundation awarded him the order of Nishan-e-Khalsa for his superb accomplishments in promoting the glory and pride of the Khalsa Panth.

Presently, he is interested in promoting Sikh Studies in North America.

Dr Harbans Lal met and married Amrita Kaur in Chicago in 1964. They now live in Arlington, Texas, and have three children. All the three children live in the United States. Sophia Kaur was born in Kansas, educated in Texas and is doing her residency in Surgery in New Jersey; Ravinder Singh was born in Rhode Island, and is currently in Paris as the Head of Business Development for Nortel, France; Ronjeet Singh was born in Rhode Island and is an electronic engineer with Fujitsu in Dallas, Texas.

Dr Harbans Lal inherited his love for the *Gurbani* from his parents, and also because of his mother's relationship with Dr Gopal Singh Dardi's family. A person who kept his interest going in the subject was the Late Principal Satbir Singh who visited him in Texas in 1982. They had known each other since 1948, and continued to remain in touch over the years. Satbir Singh made him promise that along with his scientific work, he would try to interpret the Guru's message through his articles.

Harbans Lal goes back in time to 1956.

When he first arrived in the United States on Guru Nanak's birthday, there was no one with him to celebrate the occasion. He invited a few Indian friends and took them to the college cafeteria for lunch. He also wrote an article on the Guru's life and teachings which was published in *Asian Student.* What started out as a hobby in his student days and a part-time activity while he was teaching became a full-time interest after he retired. He says, 'There is a need to explain my faith to my neighbours in the Western societies and also to clarify my own thinking on many issues. We have our *Guru Granth Sahib* with us for three centuries and we bow to its authority everyday. Let us then ask ourselves this question: "Are Sikh communities in the world truly inspired to comprehend and cherish the principles that the *Guru Granth Sahib* calls upon us to live by?"'

Dr Harbans Lal affirms: 'I am a Sikh because I found *Gurmat* most suited for my spiritual needs. I am very fortunate that the Guru permitted me to follow his path. I don't know another way that can bring me inner satisfaction.'

He also has his views on Khalistan. He says: 'In the early '40s I began to agitate for the proportional representation of Sikhs in various legislative bodies in undivided India. By 1945 I became the proponent of a much broader ideology and believed that what Sikhs needed was an environment in which they could give full expression to their Sikh nationality. They are a nation not because they rule over a land, but because they have a common mother tongue. Sikhs are a nation because of their common belief system, their common theology, and their shared concern for members with the same nationality.'

UNITED STATES OF AMERICA

Economics and Youth Camps

BIMAL KAUR AND DR BALWANT SINGH

Dr Balwant Singh, Professor Emeritus at Bucknell University is a renowned teacher of Statistics and Econometrics, and the author of many scholarly papers and books. He is also known for his work with Sikh youth since 1977. Since 1983 Dr Singh has been especially involved in the Sikh youth movement initiated by Sardar Shamsher Singh through an organization—Sri Hemkunt Foundation. Dr Singh is entrusted with the duty of selecting and procuring books on Sikhism for Sikh youth to review and write questions on, for different age groups for the International Sikh Youth Symposium held annually in various countries of the Western Hemisphere. Every year 1500–2000 Sikh boys and girls read these books and deliver speeches at zonal and national levels. His wife, Bimal Kaur is known as 'Bimal Auntie' among the second generation Sikhs in America who have attended Sikh Youth Camps in Pennsylvania, Tuskorora and New York.

Dr Singh was born on 15 August 1927 in the village of Naushera in district Sargodha, now in Pakistan. He received

Bimal Kaur and Balwant Singh share a joke.

Balwant Singh addressing a congregation of Sikh Youth at a camp.

his early education in Naushera. In 1947 he and his family migrated to Delhi in India, where he completed his undergraduate education and got his Master's degree in Economics from Punjab University in 1950. He taught at Punjab University (Camp) College for sometime and then moved to Delhi School of Economics from where he got a Master's degree in Statistics in 1959. He taught at Delhi University for sometime before migrating to the United States, and joined the University of Pennsylvania for yet another Master's degree, this time in Economics from Wharton School.

Balwant Singh was married to Bimal Kaur in 1954, and they had a son and a daughter before he left for the United States. Bimal Kaur and her children joined him two years later. They had no difficulty in adjusting to the new environment because the children were going to public schools in India where English was the primary language of instruction. Bimal started studying for a Master's degree in Arts at the University of Pennsylvania, Bloomsburg. In 1967 Balwant Singh was appointed Professor at Bucknell University from where he retired in 1993 as a Professor Emeritus.

During his tenure at Bucknell, Dr Singh had the distinction of holding the Christian R. Lindback Chair in Business Administration. He was also a visiting scholar at Cambridge University (UK) in 1979, then in 1987. In 1993 he and his wife received the Burmah-Bucknell Award for International and Inter-cultural Understanding.

Dr Singh is the author of papers on Financial Theory, Development Economics, Urban Economics and Econometrics. He was a Research Fellow with Nobel Laureate Lawrence R. Klein at the University of Pennsylvania.

On being asked whether he had faced any discrimination because of his turban and beard, Dr Singh replied, 'Never in my life did I have any difficulty finding a job. Econometrics was a new subject and I had seven different offers to choose from as soon as I started looking for a job in the United States.'

Dr Singh imbibed his emotional attachment to the Sikh faith from his grandmother when he was barely ten. She made him speak on the subject at the school assembly. He also got to meet Sant Sangat Singh of Kamaliya and remained in touch with the latter until his death.

Dr Singh started Sikh Youth Camps in Lewisburg in 1974, which were attended by prominent Sikhs from all over the country. The idea of holding Sikh Youth Camps had been mooted for a while. The first such camp was held in 1977 in Racoon Park. About 50–70 boys and girls attended the camp. Dr Singh's wife, Bimal, was the only one providing meals and snacks for the children and staff. Soon parents started to volunteer as teachers and helpers.

These camps have been instrumental in teaching the Sikh way of life to thousands of Sikh students. More importantly they have served as a support system for young Sikhs asking serious questions about retaining their Sikh identity in alien surroundings. The most serious dilemma they were faced with was about dating and marriage.

Dr Singh is most concerned about opening a dialogue in the Sikh community on this very sensitive issue.

Both his children, although full-fledged Sikhs, have married non-Sikhs. The grandchildren are being brought up as Sikhs mainly because of Bimal and Dr Singh's strong influence, but not all Sikh families in the United States can boast of such a strong and educated lineage.

Dr Singh is not in favour of Khalistan although he is of the view that the Government of India has been unfair to the Sikhs. He is, however, very optimistic about the future of Sikhs in India and abroad, because they are honest, hard-working and have self-esteem. They believe in *Chardi Kala.*

UNITED STATES OF AMERICA

Fifth Generation American

JANE SINGH

I had been hearing about Jane Singh for many years at Sikh gatherings in Washington DC. She was Jane the researcher, Jane the scholar, Jane the writer and above all, Jane the community activist. I did not get a chance to meet her earlier but had an image of Jane Singh in my mind. I assumed Jane to perhaps be a White American, married to a Sikh. When I met her in San Francisco, however, she turned out to be a tall, slender Punjabi.

Jane is a lecturer at the University of California at Berkeley, and is involved with the local South Asian Community. She is also a member of an Asian women's group called Asian Women United which publishes a variety of educational material on issues concerning Asian American women. The group has produced award-winning films, and anthologies on topics such as race, gender and social inequality in American society. Their most recent work, a book for teenaged girls, is a collection of stories, essays and poetry. Entitled *Invasian: Asian Sisters Represent,* this anthology aims to empower young women by voicing their concerns.

Jane is the youngest of Puna Singh and Nand Kaur's seven children. She was born and brought up in Northern California where her parents had settled in 1929. Jane's father came to the United States as a teenager. After working for a few years, he applied for an American citizenship which was granted to him in 1921. The following year, he returned home to visit his family and to purchase land in the canal colonies in Punjab. Later that year, he married Nand Kaur. Before the marriage he made it clear to her family that he would return with his bride to the United States.

In 1923, Puna Singh returned to the United States with Nand Kaur.

Nand Kaur describes her early years in the United States as a mixture of longing for her family and her home in Punjab, and the thrill of having new experiences in a new place.

Jane recalls that her parents and other immigrants had to face a lot of discrimination. The United States Immigration Acts passed in 1917 and 1924, made it virtually impossible for Asians to enter the United States. In 1923 the United States Supreme Court's Decision in the United States vs. Bhagat Singh Thind case, declared people of Indian origin to be non-whites and therefore not eligible to become naturalized American citizens. Due to this decision, approximately seventy people of Indian origin, including Jane's father, lost their citizenships. When the opportunity arose in the late 1920s to regain citizenship, Puna Singh refused to apply and declared that he was not interested in becoming a citizen of a country that blatantly discriminated against people because of their race.

'It was not until 1950, after many laws had changed in the United States that he became a naturalized citizen.'

Jane's parents settled on a farm in California. They remained Keshdhari Sikhs, taught their children Punjabi and instilled Sikh values in them. Thanks to her parents' determination, Jane and her siblings all speak Punjabi fluently, and have a strong sense of the Sikh-Punjabi identity.

Jane's parents were always involved in the gurdwara, and

Jane Singh's parents Puna Singh and Nand Kaur with Jane's brothers Mahinder Singh, Kirpal Singh and Pal Singh in Sacramento, California in 1930.

Jane Singh with Fellow Asian Women United board members, Eliza Chan (left) and Elaine Kim (right) at Berkeley, California in 2001.

community activities. The small Californian community of perhaps fifteen hundred Punjabis and other Indians gathered periodically to celebrate religious holidays. It gave Nand Kaur an opportunity to meet other Punjabi women, as well as Mexican and American wives of Punjabis. She became fluent in both English and Spanish. After the 1950s when the community began to grow in size, Nand Kaur became a mentor to many new immigrant women from Punjab. She would help the newcomers with their children's school admissions or accompany them on visits to doctors.

Another important part of community life during the early years was the Indian nationalist movement. In an exhibition, *Echoes of Freedom*, recently held at the University of California at Berkeley, a quote from Nand Kaur described the activities at the Stockton Sikh Temple: 'There was a three-day sequence of meetings held at the beginning of each year.' The first day was devoted to discussing topics related to education such as women's education in Punjab or reports from Punjabi educational societies; the second day focused on the Ghadar Party and its effort to gain independence for India; and the last day was marked by the celebration of the tenth Guru, Guru Gobind Singh's birth.

Jane's parents supported the Indian independence movement. Puna Singh and Nand Kaur helped by sending large sums of money to Punjab for education, and to support various social and political movements.

'How on earth did you get your name Jane?' I asked her.

She replied, 'Oh there is a story behind it. Just before I was born, my brother Puran who was about six or seven years old, convinced my parents that he should be allowed to name me. He was expecting a little brother, so when I arrived, he was taken by surprise. Not willing to miss the opportunity, he came up with the name "Jane" from one of his school books. So after the lovely Punjabi names of my elder siblings Kirpal, Pal, Mahinder, Nina, Sohan and Puran . . . came Jane.'

Being the youngest in the family, Jane was left with her

parents after all her siblings were married. The family is now in its fifth generation and mostly lives in Northern California. Jane, who is single, has close ties with each of these generations.

Jane got her first degree in Social Sciences and Education and taught at a school for a year. She returned to college to do a graduate course in South Asian Studies, eventually earning a Master's degree, then a Ph.D. However, Jane was not entirely happy with this field since the emphasis was on studying Asia from a Western perspective. After attending Agra University for a year on a Fulbright scholarship, she returned to the United States with a new idea.

'Why not study South Asians in the United States?'

Since the 1980s, Jane has done a series of projects on the South Asian experience in the United States. In 1984 she curated an exhibition, *People of South Asia in America,* that was held along with public programme across the United States. In 1991 she began teaching in the Asian American Studies Programme at the University of California.

Jane is very concerned about minority groups and the critical need in the United States to forge a true multicultural society. She knows she is different from the average mainstream American, and likes being different. She is proud of her heritage and she knows who she is. Recently she visited Punjab after almost twenty years.

'It was great to see Punjab after such a long time. Yes, there were the usual problems such as overcrowding, terrible air pollution, dramatic social and economic inequities, but the vitality of the region and the people is so evident. If only there was a way to create the needed public works, good jobs and better schools, nothing would curb the energy and will of the people. One can only hope for good leadership and greater stability in the area.'

During her four-week stay in Punjab, Jane visited the ancestral village in Jalandhar district. 'If you want to feel your roots and a sense of history, just go home to your village.' She also attended part of a workshop on Punjab in Chandigarh that was sponsored by the University of California, Santa Barbara and Columbia University.

'There were lots of excellent Punjabi academicians discussing topics ranging from History to Economics to Culture. The best part of the trip was the time spent with family and friends. There is a kind of intensity in relationships and family life that exists here. People here are busy as well but not constantly running about as we tend to do in the West. And it was nice to hear Punjabi being spoken a lot, even by the diehard English language speakers.'

How did Jane react to the demand for Khalistan? She replied: 'My family was outraged by what happened to the Sikhs in 1984. Since there had always been such a commitment to Indian Independence amongst Sikhs in the United States, the events of 1984 felt like a tremendous betrayal. I think that many amongst the Sikhs diaspora feel the need for more regional and state autonomy for Punjab rather than for a completely separate Khalistan or Punjab. Perhaps the nation needs to redefine itself as a country. In my understanding India originally saw itself as a federation of states. The subcontinent contains such a diversity of languages and cultures, much like Europe. If each state was allowed to develop more freely, there would be greater potential for more rapid development.'

Jane is disappointed with the leaders thrown up by the Sikh community.

'My impression is that most people of the diaspora, and maybe even in Punjab, are very skeptical about the leadership. Wise and selfless leaders would certainly improve both local and global conditions of Sikhs and others. But then, such leaders are a rare breed in any part of the world,' she says.

However, she predicts a brighter future for American Sikhs.

'In the United States and other parts of the world, Sikhs are flourishing. I think the challenge lies in Sikhs acting as a group and in coalition with other communities to ensure that everyone has access to a clean environment, good schools and jobs, and equal opportunities.'

From the Aroma of Chandigarh to the Cherry Blossoms of Washington

RANJU AND BRYJINDER SINGH KOHLI

Bryjinder Singh Kohli is the first-born of the late Sardar Darshan Singh Kohli—the founder–proprietor of Aroma Hotel in Chandigarh. He was born in 1950 in Firozabad, Uttar Pradesh, where his father was a contractor of coal ash with the Indian Railways. Darshan Singh's family owned several businesses jointly. Aroma Hotel was one of them. His family came to Chandigarh in 1970 to take charge of the running of the hotel.

'Aroma was built in 1955 and in that sense, the Kohlis can be termed as one of the pioneering families of Chandigarh,' says Bryjinder with a sense of pride.

Bryjinder's earliest memory goes back to his schooldays at La Martiniere's in Lucknow. His father who originally belonged to Rawalpindi lost all he had during Partition and was trying to re establish himself in India. Though short of money, Darshan Singh was determined to give the best education to his children. Bryjinder was sent to a boarding school in Lucknow.

Left: Ranju and Bryjinder Singh Kohli cut a perfect picture of togetherness. Below: A lover of music, Bryjinder Singh Kohli is a fan of Nusrat Fateh Ali Khan.

Bryjinder Singh Kohli likes to punctuate his interest in cherry blossoms with his passion for golf.

He remembers a time when his parents did not have money to send him with the school team to Calcutta to play Rugby Football. Desperate to go, Bryjinder turned a deaf ear to his mother's entreaties. Then his father came in with all the cash he had, placed it on a table and told his son to take what he needed, but to leave a five-rupee note so that he could pay his bus fare back home.

'The memory of that event has stayed with me,' says Bryjinder. His father has been his role model. He built his business for the family. They lived well. While they enjoyed all the luxuries of life, he took a rickshaw to the hotel or went on foot.

After getting a Bachelor's degree from Shri Ram College of Commerce, Bryjinder travelled far and wide. He showed no interest in the family business, nor any signs of getting married and settling down. His younger brother Manmohan Singh married a girl of his choice. A family friend, Justice Harbans Singh (Retired Chief Justice of the Punjab and Haryana High Court) noticed his potential. He also knew Sardar Jodh Singh of All India Radio, Jalandhar, whose granddaughter was of marriageable age. He suggested the match and within a month Bryjinder and Ranju were married.

The decision to migrate to the United States was made over a period of time. Ranju was not happy being just a wife and daughter-in-law. When Ranju and Bryjinder visited the United States for the second time after their marriage in 1984, they watched on television the horrors of anti-Sikh riots in India following Mrs Indira Gandhi's assassination. Ranju felt America offered her an opportunity to find her true identity. So in spite of a well-established family business in India, Ranju and Bryjinder made their final move to the United States in 1987.

Unlike most immigrants who had to struggle a lot before they found their foothold in America, Bryjinder and Ranju got early breaks in their professions. Bryjinder was hired by the Yellow Pages publishing company as the Area Manager.

'Did your turban pose a hindrance in getting your first job?' I asked.

'On the contrary, the turban is something that attracts attention. Race is at times an issue, never religion,' replied Bryjinder.

Bryjinder is the National Distribution Manager for the same company.

'What is the secret of your success?' I asked him.

'*Allah Mehrban, Gadha Pehalwan* (When God is merciful, even a donkey becomes a champ),' was his quick answer. Bryjinder has a sense of humour and does not mind laughing at himself. On a more serious note he says, 'This job required someone streetsmart, who had run a business in India. I was prepared for the challenge. Of course, it means a lot of hard work. On most days I have to drive over 200 miles to make sure that the work is done effectively.'

He has been recognized for his diligence work and has been given a Special Recognition for Outstanding Service award.

Bryjinder is also an avid golfer. The twice-yearly tournaments attract golfers of Indian origin from as far as Chicago and San Francisco. He is conspicuous by his presence and his absence (when he decides to stay home to look after his son who has been diagnosed with autism). He is very well read, a lover of art and Urdu poetry. This is evident from his elegant home in Great Falls, Virginia, one of the more sought after suburbs of Washington. Oil paintings and antique icons adorn the walls of his living room. His favourite painting is that of Maharaja Ranjit Singh holding his durbar—one that Bryjinder had commissioned in 1998.

Bryjinder feels nostalgic about the streets of Lucknow, Delhi and Chandigarh. 'When the leaves fall, they head towards their roots,' he quotes a Chinese philosopher. He dreams of returning to India but feels that his autistic son needs to stay on in the United States and have his parents around.

Ranju has also done well during the 14 years that she has

been in the United States. She started her career with an entry-level job in a telecommunications company.

'It was like a peon's job, but a technical one,' she says.

The hiring manager told her associate, 'The girl is too smart. I don't know how long she will stick to this job,' Ranju recalls. He was right. Ranju started discovering her talents, found that she was good with computers, took evening classes and was soon on her way up. 'Today I am a Business Analyst in the IT division of the second largest telecom company in the United States.'

They moved to an expensive suburb so that their daughters could go to the best possible schools. Their efforts are paying off. Their daughter Sitara graduated with straight A's from the prestigious Langley High School, and now attends Business School at Georgetown University. The younger one, Tarranum is in eleventh grade at Langley, and is following in her sister's footsteps.

I asked Ranju and Bryjinder about their opinion on the various issues Sikhs need to deal with.

'We are a minority community and need to educate the mainstream Americans about who Sikhs are. People ask if we are Hindus or Muslims, and when we say "Neither," they say, "Then what are you?" After the 11 September attacks on the World Trade Center, we really need to educate the people about Sikhs. Anyone wearing a turban is equated with Osama bin Laden.'

Bryjinder feels the demand for Khalistan was created by frustrated politicians. Like Frankenstein's monster, it became stronger than it creator. His wife and he feel strongly that Khalistan is not a feasible option for Sikhs.

'Sikhs have sacrificed so much during the freedom struggle. They were in the forefront during all the wars. We have as much right over India as anyone else. Why confine ourselves to just a small state?'

UNITED STATES OF AMERICA

From Poverty to Top Taxpayer

PUSHPINDER KAUR AND BALDEV SINGH

Baldev Singh was born on 15 August 1939 in village Majatri, in Ropar district. A few years later India would celebrate its Independence on the same day. He was the eldest of the five children of an illiterate farmer, Bakhtavar Singh. His mother Prem Kaur died when he was in the eighth grade. Baldev and his three younger brothers dropped out of school because of the family's poverty.

Baldev Singh, the highest taxpayer in Howard County, Maryland in the United States today, recalls the days when he had to walk four-and-a-half miles each way to attend school in Kharar, in Ambala district. When his mother died, he had to cook, clean, and wash clothes for his younger brothers. Poverty and neglect marked his life until 1960 when he moved to Chandigarh to teach in a High School.

He taught in District Board schools, and worked towards his college degree privately. While teaching in a government High School, he joined Law College in Chandigarh and got his LL.B. degree in 1966. He was the first of his

Beside every successful man is a woman—Baldev Singh with his wife Pushpinder Kaur.

Baldev Singh and Pushpinder Kaur share their moment in the sun.

sixteen cousins and siblings to have graduated, and become a lawyer.

Baldev Singh had just started his legal practice when he came in contact with the Akali leader Sant Fateh Singh who launched the agitation for a Punjabi Suba.

G.S. Tohra was leading a procession from Amritsar to Chandigarh. The procession was aimed at raising awareness among the masses about Chandigarh, and Punjab's claim on it as the capital of Punjab. On the way Tohra and his associates had to stop at the village Todar Majra. Baldev Singh who had by then acquired a spacious bungalow in village Kharar in district Ropar played host to the Akali leaders. Before they could reach Chandigarh, they, including Baldev Singh, were arrested and sent to Patiala Jail.

The 1967 elections were due. Baldev Singh was given the Akali party ticket from Kharar. It was traditionally a Congress constituency with a Hindu majority. The sitting member was a Sikh minister, Niranjan Singh Talib who was expected to be re-elected with a comfortable margin. Baldev Singh surprised the Congress as well as the Akalis by winning the elections hands down.

Joginder Singh Maan was the Speaker of the House; Baldev Singh was elected Deputy Speaker. He was not able to complete his term as the Punjab Assembly was dissolved by the Central Government.

In the stormy three years of the Punjab Assembly, Baldev Singh was instrumental in getting the Punjabi Bill (making Punjabi the language of the State) passed during Lachman Singh Gill's tenure as the Chief Minister of Punjab.

Early in 1970 Baldev Singh chanced to meet the American Ambassador, Chester Bowles who had been closely following the political developments in Punjab. He complimented Baldev Singh on the pivotal role he had played in having the Punjabi Bill passed amidst squabbles between the Congress, Jan Sangh and within the Akali Party, and asked him about his future plans. Baldev Singh told him that he was not cut out for politics and planned to quit.

'How about migrating to the United States?' he asked Baldev Singh.

Without thinking seriously about the implications, he answered, 'Why not?'

In three months Chester Bowles got Baldev Singh's clearance to emigrate to the United States.

Baldev Singh landed in New York in 1970. Jobs were hard to come by. Baldev Singh was willing to take up any job that could sustain him, but employers found him overqualified. Finally he found a clerical job with Metropolitan Life Insurance Company. In 1980 he was appointed the manager of a department where 36 employees reported to him. In 1983, he resigned from the post to start his own business.

I had heard him speak at Richmond Hill Gurdwara some years ago. So I asked him if he took any interest in the affairs of his community. He shifted gears.

In 1976 when he was still climbing the ladder in Metropolitan Life, the management of Richmond Hill Gurdwara offered him the Vice Chairmanship of the gurdwara. The following years he was elected as its General Secretary, a position he held until 1991, when he decided to shift to Maryland to start his own business.

'I had dreamt of making this gurdwara in Richmond Hill the most important Sikh shrine in the Western Hemisphere,' said Baldev Singh. He invited Sikh leaders and prominent *raagi jathas* from India to the gurdwara. He coordinated their itinerary with gurdwaras on the West Coast, for instance, in Yuba City, Stockton, Los Angeles so that they could grace most of the gurdwaras in this country with their presence.

'I wanted to honour distinguished and talented raagis like Professor Darshan Singh, Bhai Avtar Singh and the late Bhai Dharam Singh Zakhmi. Mrs Indira Gandhi visited the gurdwara in the early 1980s as did some eminent Americans.'

The highlight of Baldev Singh's tenure was the beginning of the Baisakhi Parade in New York in 1986 when Baldev Singh was elected Master of Ceremonies.

'Thousands of Americans joined the parade to partake in the Guru ka langar. We served food afterwards,' said Baldev Singh. 'I had told the *sangat* at the gurdwara to turn up in their smartest clothes befitting the Khalsa.'

Baldev Singh recalls the tumultuous years of the 1980s when Punjab was in the grip of terrorism and anti-Sikh violence had erupted in Indian cities following the assassination of Mrs Gandhi. Thousands of young Sikhs migrated to the United States, and were housed and fed in gurdwaras till they found jobs.

In 1991 Baldev Singh resigned from his job at Metropolitan Life and bought a truck stop in Maryland.

'It can now park 650 trucks, has a hotel with 110 rooms and a restaurant that can seat 185 persons. It is a town by itself in Jessup, Maryland,' he added.

He made enough money from that truck stop to buy three gas stations, and a family estate in Clarkesville for his second wife Pushpinder and himself. His first marriage had ended in a divorce during the transition between New York and Maryland. Baldev's son from his first marriage has a lucrative business of his own.

In 1997, Baldev Singh married Pushpinder Kaur, who left a well-paid job at a leading financial corporation to join him in Maryland. They both live in an elegant, custom-built home in Clarkesville. Pushpinder manages a gas station and a subway restaurant. The gas station has an eatery that Pushpinder looks after as well.

Baldev and Pushpinder (known as Juju to her friends) feel blessed for the turn in their fortunes. They have much in common—those unforgettable days of want in Punjab and the struggle for survival when they came to New York. They want to give something back to their community, and are building a school in village Majatri, Baldev Singh's ancestral village. They have already spent Rs 400,000 in building the local school comprising eight classrooms, staff quarters, a library and sports grounds. They are keen to build a community hall for the village, where people can discuss their affairs and relax. They also plan to build a medical dispensary which will not be dependant on government support.

Baldev Singh is very critical of Sikh leadership in Punjab. 'Their corrupt practices and skulduggery upsets me,' says he. He is also distressed with the complacency Sikh religious leaders have shown in the wake of mass female feticide in Punjab. He feels that the Akal Takht should issue edicts against such evil practices which in the coming decades are likely to result in a social imbalance difficult to remedy.

UNITED STATES OF AMERICA

Community Service

MIRIN AND TEJBIR SINGH PHOOL

Guru Nanak Foundation of America (GNFA) is among the oldest Sikh shrines in the Washington DC metropolitan area. In 1970 when the gurdwara was founded there were about seventy-five Sikh families in the area and the number of Sikhs in the Sunday congregation did not exceed a few dozens. Today the gurdwara can barely accommodate the thousands of Sikhs who turn up every Sunday from the tristate area. So every Sunday, the gurdwara management holds two main *diwans* instead of just one.

The morning service begins at 7.30 a.m. sharp and ends at 9.30 a.m. followed by breakfast for the entire gathering. The second service starts at 11.30 a.m. and carries on till 1.30 p.m. Local leaders make speeches. At times Dr G.S. Aulakh reminds the Sikh community of the need for Khalistan. At other times visiting politicians or scholars collect funds for the welfare of the poor living in the remote villages of Punjab. Those who enjoy listening to Asa di war kirtan being performed by the raagi jatha of Bhai Jagmohan Singh and Hermohan Singh, prefer to attend the morning service.

The young man coordinating the service with the help of his two children and others, is Tejbir Singh Phool. His two children play the harmonium and sing the Gurbani because they know a lot of it by rote. Tejbir's wife Mirin is an elegant young lady who shares her husband's enthusiasm for community service.

I asked Mirin and Tejbir what set their children apart from others. They replied, 'Why don't you ask them?'

So I put a simple question to twelve-year-old Bishan Singh, 'Why do you come to the gurdwara? Do you understand anything that goes on?'

He replied: 'I come to the gurdwara because I like it. I learnt how to read and write Gurmukhi. I learnt kirtan at Sunday school. I do not understand all that goes on but my father explains everything to Samina and me on our way back home.'

'How long have you been to school in America and how many Sikhs are there in your class?'

He replied 'I am in seventh grade and have gone to school in America since kindergarten. I am the only Sikh in my class with a *pugri.*'

I asked him, 'Do you have to answer many questions about your religion?'

He replied hesitatingly, 'No . . . yes. I am asked more questions than others, but I know how to answer them. If they ask me why I wear a turban, I tell them that I have long unshorn hair, and wear a turban because I have to keep my head covered. If they ask me why I wear a *kara* I tell them it is a reminder for me to not do wrong things. Sometimes they ask me how long my hair is?'

'Do American students make fun of you because you look different?' I asked diffidently.

'Nobody makes fun of me. They only ask questions,' replied Bishan. 'My friends support me. Once I went to attend a camp with American kids. When I took off my turban at night, they saw how long my hair was and exclaimed, "Oh my God!"'

'I heard you reciting your prayers. What do they mean to you?' I asked.

Tejbir Singh Phool with his wife Mirin and their two children Bishan and Samina.

The author, Dr Surjit Kaur listens to Tejbir Singh Phool expressing his views on the future of Sikhism in the West.

'Doing paath makes me feel strong, safe and good,' was his reply.

'Who are your friends?'s

'They are Indians, Pakistanis, Koreans, Chinese and Americans.'

'Do you ever go to India?'

'Yes, we go back to India almost once every two years. Last year we went to Delhi, then to Punjab to visit the Golden Temple at Amritsar. We were there early at 3.00 a.m. to watch the *Guru Granth Sahib* being brought from the Akal Takht Sahib to Sri Harmandir Sahib. It was lovely to watch the reflection of the stars and the moon in the holy tank surrounding the Golden Temple. Then we went to a gurdwara built by Guru Amardas. There are eighty-four steps to go down to Baoli Sahib to do *ishnan*. We also visited Anandpur Sahib and saw Guru Gobind Singh's arrow. It was fun. I would like to go back every year, but the weather is a problem.'

His sister Samina who is two year younger is more casual about the whole thing and agreed with what Bishan had to say. She wants to become a doctor when she grows up whereas Bishan would like to become a computer engineer.

Tejbir stood at a short distance with his back towards us listening to everything his children were saying. By now he had become involved with the interview and sat down to answer my questions.

'Tell me about yourself, your childhood days, your education, your marriage to Mirin and your decision to come away to the United States.'

'I was born and brought up in New Delhi. Then my parents moved to Bangkok (Tejbir's father worked with Air India), and I stayed back with my grandparents in New Delhi. My maternal grandmother took care of me and taught me the Sikh way of life. I did my MBA in Delhi, then went to Canada where I did my Master's in Economics. After that I came back to India and got married to Mirin, landed a job with the World Bank and moved to Washington DC.' Tejbir is currently working as an Advisor to the World Bank.

'What does your wife Mirin do?' I asked.

'She has her own business, a beauty salon,' he replied.

Mirin wears her long hair in a French twist and looks like a fashion model. She also comes from New Delhi but has lived in many countries around the world because her father served in the World Health Organization. Now he is retired and the family lives in Washington DC.

Tejbir and Mirin are a young couple in their thirties. They have everything going for them—money, prestige, looks. They move in the highest society in the Washington DC. metropolitan area. And somewhere along the line they have made a conscious decision to give utmost importance to the upbringing of their children. Their social life revolves around a few like-minded couples who spend most of their evenings and weekends transporting their children to the gurdwara, to kirtan and Punjabi classes and perhaps to schools if the children are involved in sports and other extra-curricular activities. When they get together for an evening dinner or weekend picnic parties, they bring their children along and the children usually have their own little pizza parties away from the adults. Adults and children alike are indifferent to the social, economic or even political situation in Punjab.

In 2000, Sikhs of Washington DC metropolitan area were to host the International Youth Symposium on behalf of Shri Hemkunt Foundation. Sikhs from around the world flocked to Washington DC. Tejbir and Mirin had to arrange for the symposium, boarding and lodging, sightseeing for the out-of-town guests, and most of all, for the final evening function and the banquet. Mirin was asked to coordinate hotel arrangements, and Tejbir pledged the highest donation—$3,000—for the purpose.

At the final function where everyone invited was present, Tejbir and Mirin were conspicuous by their absence.

UNITED STATES OF AMERICA

Gurbani in the United States

BIBI AMARJIT KAUR

Kirtan or hymn singing is an integral part of every Sikh ritual since the *Guru Granth Sahib's* hymns are all set to ragas of Indian classical music. In India every city has scores of professional raagi jathas. Sikh families living abroad and have to make do with the services of visiting raagis or the taped Gurbani. Amarjit Kaur has a jatha comprising two sisters and a brother.

Hardly eighteen Bibi Amarjit came to the United States on the invitation of Yogi Harbhajan Singh. Her brief was to teach the Gurbani kirtan and Punjabi to American Sikhs. She brought her sister Balbir Kaur and brother Onkar Singh with her to complete her raagi jatha. Her brother was an accomplished tabla master and had accompanied singers of the calibre of Mehdi Hassan, Ghulam Ali and Mallika Pukhraj. Unfortunately Onkar Singh died suddenly two years ago while he was reciting the evening prayer—*Rehras*—with Amarjit and the family. Since then Amarjit's husband, Jagjit Singh Rathore (Jaggi) has learnt to play the tabla for the jatha.

'Onkar, my little brother was a great artist, it was a joy to accompany him,' says Amarjit. 'But Jaggi is thoughtful. Now he is learning my style, and perhaps I will not miss Onkar's tabla as much.'

Amarjit was born and brought up in Delhi where her father was a government architect. He also did voluntary work designing temples and gurdwaras. Accompanied by her sister, Balbir, Amarjit started singing the Gurbani. She also learnt kirtan, and was invited to sing at the Rashtrapati Bhawan by President Zakir Hussain. Yogi Bhajan was a family friend, which is how Amarjit was invited to come to the United States.

Once in the United States, Amarjit travelled to various ashrams where Yogi Bhajan taught yoga to Americans. She taught Gurbani and kirtan to his disciples. This went on for quite a few years before she met Jagjit Singh Rathore in Washington. They returned to India, got married with the blessings of Amarjit's parents.

Amarjit and Jagjit have a lovely daughter, Sahiba Kaur, who is now nineteen, and sings the Gurbani with her mother. She is good at her studies and keen on becoming a doctor. When I asked her about marriage, she replied, 'Yes I do want to get married. I will marry a Gursikh and someone my parents choose for me.'

'Are you serious?' I asked in astonishment.

'Yes, Auntie, I am serious. I don't want to know my husband before marriage. I want to get married in the traditional Punjabi way.'

Bibi Amarjit Kaur has a word with Yogi Bhajan in between singing the Gurbani.

UNITED STATES OF AMERICA

Proud of being Sikh and American

SANDIP SINGH

Sandip Singh was born on 25 November 1977 in Jersey City. His parents had migrated to the United States in 1971 when immigration laws were changed to welcome professionals. He earned his six-year Doctor of Pharmacy degree (Pharm. D.) at Rutgers University in New Brunswick, New Jersey. From the start he intended to apply his clinical knowledge for networking and writing. He is currently on a Post-doctoral Industrial Fellowship in Marketing Research at Ortho Biotech of Johnson & Johnson. His job requires a lot of travelling as he conducts training programmes around the country.

In the early 1980s, in a small town called New Milford in New Jersey, Sandip was the only Sikh student wearing a *patka* and an eye patch to correct a lazy eye. He learnt to fend for himself. He was good-looking, athletic and did very well in his studies. I asked him how he coped with his fellow-students who could at times be uncouth and rough. He replied, 'Being a Sikh who wore a patch on his eye for two years, I went through my fair share of trials and tribulations. There were many occasions on which I had to explain why I looked different. I was usually able to bring them round by telling them that Sikhism is a major religion, and there are more Sikhs in the world than Jews. Sikhism's belief in religious equality is of paramount importance to me.'

At times his audience is not too receptive to what he has to say about Sikhism. 'These are often losing battles,' he admits. 'The only way to win is to accept that some people refuse to be educated on anything that is not connected with their business. I just forget about them.'

He related an episode. When he went to a bar in college, he was refused entry. The bouncer thought he was wearing a hat. Sandip explained that it was a turban, not a hat. The bouncer refused to listen. Sandip asked to speak to his manager. The bouncer replied that the manager was busy, and asking Sandip to get lost, pushed him out. Sandip wrote about the incident in the school magazine. That did a lot to inform students about Sikhism.

Sandip Singh currently works in Marketing Research with Johnson & Johnson. Apart from having to meet likely customers, he has to see men and women working in different departments, many of whom are in senior positions. For the most part, he says, he found his looking different to be an advantage. 'I am easily recognizable and I dress better than most of them. I take a keen interest in my job and have a sense of humour. These take you a long way in a corporate environment,' he said. Occasionally, he realized that his colleagues didn't even know that he was of Indian origin, leave alone who a Sikh was. Sandeep feels, however, that though in urban areas people are concerned about difference of race and religion, they are gradually overcoming their prejudices.

Sandip is very optimistic about the future of Sikhs in the United States. 'Many Sikhs have done very well for themselves. My only fear is that the second and third generations of Sikh Americans may forget the values our emigrant forefathers

Sandeep Singh takes immense pride in being a Sikh and an American.

cherished. Besides that, as long as they continue to work hard and earn an honest living, they will flourish in America,' said Sandip, adding, 'Sikhs are even better off in America than in India. Though I have never faced any discrimination when I've visited India, I have heard a lot of sordid tales from other Sikhs.

'Do I feel like an equal to white Americans? The answer is, yes... at almost all levels of my life I can relate to my white friends. Being a Sikh does not make me feel any less acceptable than a Hispanic, East Asian, Muslim or Jew.'

Sandip likes to visit his ancestral country whenever he can. Most members of his extended family live in Punjab and he wants to retain his links with them. He also likes to visit Sikh pilgrim centres to refresh his faith. He adds, 'I was born in America and have lived here all my life. I am an American. I have more in common with Americans than I do with Indians. I don't see that as a problem. There are many white American Sikhs in this country. Sikhism is a religion, not a culture, and I strongly believe in that. Sikhism will never become a global religion until people realize that. The adversity I experienced as a kid has made me a stronger person. I am committed to preserving my Sikh heritage. There is a large amount of prejudice against certain other religions, and gender discrimination as well. None of these are justified. I do not subscribe to any of them, which is why I can hold my head high and say I am as proud of being a Sikh as I am of being an American.'

UNITED STATES OF AMERICA

Spreading Guru Nanak's Message in the Western World

SHAKTA KAUR AND KARTAR SINGH KHALSA

White American Sikhs constitute a community of their own. Both men and women wear white clothes and sport turbans. They have their own gurdwaras but maintain close links with Indian Sikhs.

Shakta Kaur Khalsa, as she is know in the Indian circles, was born and bought up in a blue-collar family in Pittsburgh. She was the first-born, and her mother named her April, and April Meyers she was till Yogi Bhajan gave her the name she proudly goes by today.

Shakta did not agree with the way her parents looked at things and people. They were Protestants and went to the Baptist United Methodist Church. Shakta says, 'If Jesus were the only way to God, what about non-Christians—Muslims, Hindus, Buddhists, and Sikhs?'

She heard her parents squabbling and swearing at each other. Till the age of four, she was a strict vegetarian. Dinner was a eternal struggle, with her parents trying to force-feed her, till they realized that she wouldn't eat anything that was 'flesh'.

Kartar Singh Khalsa has found his centre in the Sikh Dharma.

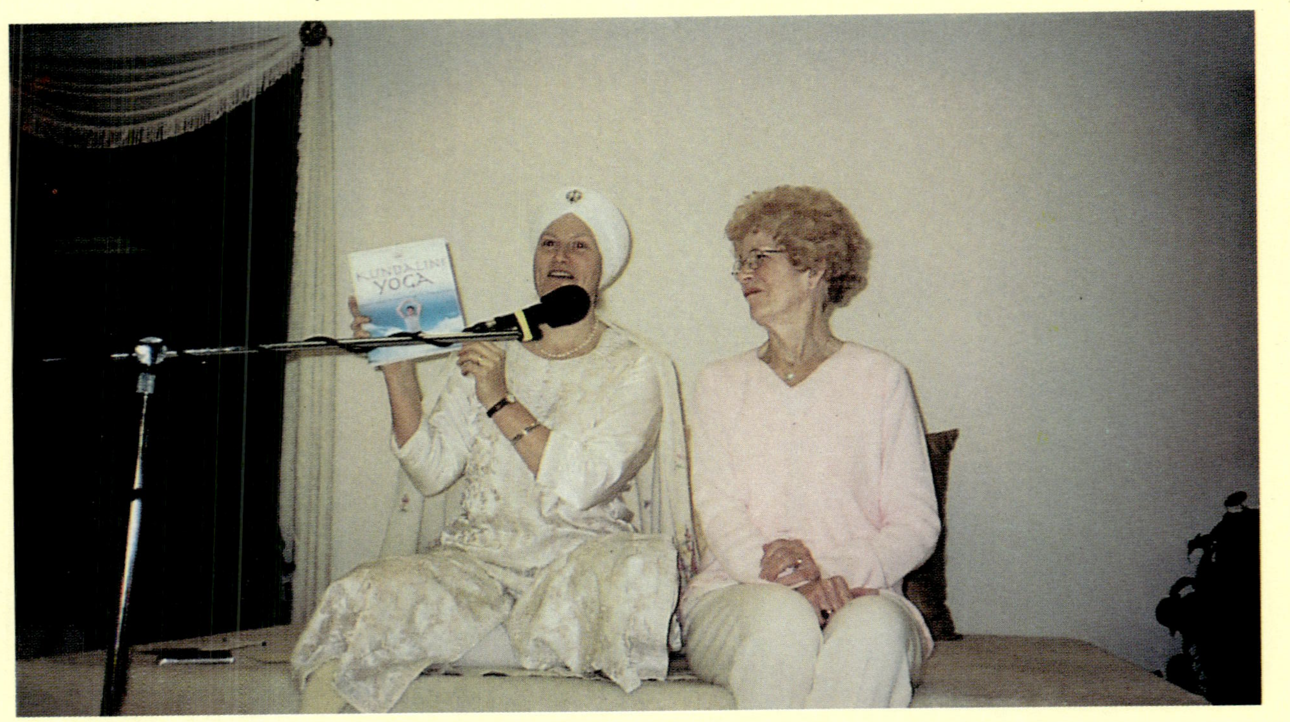

Shakta Kaur and her mother Mrs Meyers at the release of Shakta Kaur's book on Kundalini Yoga.

Shakta believes her vegetarianism has something to do with her previous incarnation—she must have been a native of India.

Shakta graduated from High School in 1968.

'All my relatives were German, and our friends were Europeans. I enjoyed being with people but did not like working with machines,' said Shakta. She was talking of the time when she had taken up a job as a telephone operator immediately after High School. In her free time she wrote poems which she preserved for a long time before she met her future husband, Kartar Singh and handed over the volume to him.

Before she met Kartar Singh, April had been experimenting with marijuana and LSD—considered by many as mind-expanding drugs—in search of a spiritual experience. During this time she met a man from Venezuela—a diplomat nine years older than her. They were engaged for three years. April broke the engagement because she felt there was more to life than going to parties, and ballroom dancing.

Her quest for spirituality brought her to the doorsteps of an ashram where men and women lived together as a cohesive group, helping each other. There she learned the Kundalini Yoga and became so proficient in it that she went on to first write books on yoga for children, then later for adults. She recalls the experience in the ashram, 'We helped each other get up early and do sadhana, a way of raising consciousness through prayer, yoga, meditation and devotional singing. Sadhana started at 4 a.m. and carried on for two-and-a-half hours. It is a very rigorous life, which is why there are so few of us but Yogi Bhajan keeps adding to the numbers. Someone in the ashram said that if you were to do what Yogi Bhajan tells you to do, you would need a day that is five days long...'

'Does Yogi Bhajan practice what he preaches?' I asked. Shakta burst out laughing, and said, 'I am not going to say anything, you will have to ask him about that.'

She still recalls her days in the ashram, 'We sat on hard cold floors, took cold showers. It was the Guru Gobind Singh type of energy. You had to be strong. There she also learnt the concept of *sewa.* Once a month she had to cook breakfast and pack lunch for over fifteen people who worked outside the ashram. They worked hard and ate huge meals. She learnt about *simran.* 'Recitation of the Gurbani brings about changes in your brain cells,' she says with a lot of conviction. And she learnt about *bana.* 'I traded my jeans and paisley jacket for bana, which literally means 'radiance'. And radiant we were in our white clothes and turbans. A simple trip to the shopping mall, for instance, meant being stared at by just about ever passer-by. Children would often point fingers and say, "Hey Diaper-head." Those days one felt safer going out in groups. These insults don't bother me anymore.'

During the days Shakta Kaur worked at the Golden Temple Café in Baltimore, and it was here that she met Kartar Singh who was in charge of the Grocery Store. 'I first loved him because he made me laugh. I loved him enough to marry him because I saw he was the finest and most steadfast person I had ever met. He had dignity, generosity, and the capacity to forgive. He was calm, cool and collected, which drove me crazy at times, but still one of the main attractions for my fly-off-the-handle, spontaneous personality.'

Shakta Kaur was baptized at the age of twenty-six. She kicked her drug addiction and found ecstasy in prayer. She and Kartar Singh got married along with eight other couples, and were blessed by Yogi Bhajan. And they have been married for over twenty-five years now.

Now when she looks back and analyses things more objectively, she realizes that it was due to her general discontentment with life that she wanted a child. Even after twelve years of marriage she had not conceived. She also had doubts about her future. She no longer wanted to keep herself away from the mainstream American life, but wanted be a part of it. All that was going to happen but she had to be patient.

Kartar Singh was born in Illinois in a middle-class family.

He was the oldest of five children of the Camdys. His parents named him James. Born into a Catholic family, James wanted to become a priest, and was always involved with the church. As an altar boy, he would rise early and drive to church for the early morning mass. It was during that period as he was getting ready to graduate from High School—that he decided against priesthood, and joined the Notre Dame University to study law. He went to Austria for a while. It was during his stay there that he changed his attitude towards religion. He stopped going to confession.

'Then came the Civil Rights Movement. It became a passion as I was opposed to the Vietnam War. I quit college to go in for teaching English at a girls' school. Although the students were happy with me, the Principal, somehow, did not like me and did not renew the contract for a second year of teaching in that school,' he added.

James decided to join Vasta, a domestic Peace Corps, and worked with a law office helping poor people prepare their legal cases. He also worked with labour unions. None all of this was able to sustain his interest though, and after some time, he looked for a simpler and less stressful life.

He made friends with the American Sikhs working at the Golden Temple Store in Baltimore.

'Everytime something bothered me, I would land up there.'

James asked an American Sikh friend if he could come to the early morning sessions. The friend had no problem as long as James got up at 2.30 a.m., took a cold shower, and showed up at his house by 3.30 a.m.

'I enjoyed their morning sessions. They recited the Japji, then they did yoga and played the guitar. After that they had breakfast, then went back to the health-food store. Then there was a retreat in New Mexico. I went there. The *Guru Granth Sahib* had been kept in an attic—three volumes of the English translation. During the break from work I would go and read some paragraphs. I realized that whenever something bothered me, I would go to that room, and read for an hour or so. It was most helpful. This reading from the *Guru Granth Sahib* was what really worked. This was a real breakthrough in working with my mind.'

James did this for forty days while in New Mexico. He also practised Tantric Yoga to get rid of his 'neurotic self'. Shakta Kaur added, 'There are three types of Tantric Yoga—black (witchcraft), red (sexual), and white (spiritual). We only do white yoga. This yoga helps you get rid of all the subconscious blocks.'

Then James moved into the ashram. His break with his family had come much earlier. Today his parents know that James has become Kartar Singh, grown a long beard, and wears a turban.

Kartar Singh was thirty-one and Shakta Kaur was twenty-six when they got married. After twelve years they had a son. Bhajan Yogi named him Ram Dass Singh.

Ram Dass Singh went to a Khalsa school in Herndon, Virginia at the age of two-and-a-half. Then he joined a school with the mainstream American children. Looking different was not a problem with him.

'We had prepared him for that, he never came home crying, and made friends easily. He knew he was "wearing a crown on his head". Now he is nine and goes to the Miri Piri Academy in Amritsar and is very happy there. He is learning some amazing things about Sikhism.'

This was the right moment to ask them about their role in Sikh affairs, and their vision of the future.

Both are members of the Khalsa Council that comprises eighty ministers who meet twice a year—in Los Angeles on Baisakhi and in New Mexico in the fall—to look into the affairs of the *Khalsa panth*.

'We spend two years on each topic. This time the topic is: "Community leadership, Human development, and Personal Relationships." '

'How do you feel about Indian Sikhs coming to your gurdwaras? Why do you think they are attracted to the American Sikh gurdwara?' I asked them.

'Indian Sikhs are attracted to our gurdwara because there is no politics, no speeches, no conflicts,' they replied.

'What are your views on Punjab and Khalistan?' I asked.

'If you want to know how we felt about 1984—it took us a long time to know how terrible things were at that time. I remember the articles in *Time* magazine, and then Yogi Bhajan's speech—when he couldn't even talk because he was crying so much. He called a conference of all the Sikhs in the area. Many wanted to retaliate, but Yogi knew how to pacify them,' he replied.

'Khalistan?'

'It is a distraction. It is best to stick to Guru Nanak. Our true mission and purpose is to spread the Guru's word throughout the world. The time for having a small enclave (that is Punjab State for Khalistan) is over. What is needed today is team approach.'

'Is it easy or difficult for American Sikhs to find jobs in the mainstream American institutions?' I asked.

Kartar Singh replied, 'There are over eighteen thousand American Sikh families in Europe, Australia and in the cities of North America. They are highly educated people working as lawyers, teachers and doctors. They have their own businesses, for instance, Akal Security Inc. Their armed guards wearing turbans, work in Federal Courts, embassies and silver mines in the Southwest. Since they are trustworthy people, they get a lot of security contracts.

'We also have our tea business. This is the second largest business in the nation. We manufacture forty different kinds of Ayurvedic teas. We are the largest manufacturers of cereals. I am working on the marketing strategies for both these products, and make a very good salary. Shakta Kaur gets royalties from her books on Yoga. We are a prosperous community. I must mention Sunder Singh—a Khalsa of Chinese origin, who owns seven jewellery stores in this area. I have been marketing his diamond jewellery as well for quite sometime.'

My last question was to Shakta Kaur, 'What does it mean to be a Sikh? What is your relationship with your Guru, and with your teacher Yogi Bhajan?'

She replied, 'Now I know that I can do whatever I want to, in this world and still be a Sikh. My turban is like the Guru's protective hand on my head. I have a special relationship with the *Guru Granth Sahib.* I can read Gurmukhi and understand paath. I read the vaak and know what the Guru wants me to do. We all have a special relationship with Guru Ram Dass. Once while meditating Yogi Bhajan had a vision of him. That is how he was called upon to spread Guru Nanak's message in the Western world.'

UNITED STATES OF AMERICA

Trading in Style

PAMMY AND NANAK KOHLI

Nanak Kohli is one of the richest Indians (and Sikhs living in a mansion in one of the suburbs of Washington DC metropolitan area. Unlike others, he came to the United States not to make money but to spend it. He ended up making even more money. His profession is international trade and he supplies goods to almost all European countries and to India. In return he imports goods to the United States. He appears to apply that formula of trade in friendship and human relationships and he succeeds, 'Give them what they need and get what you want out of them.'

Nanak Kohli knows his trade through and through and he is adept at dealing with the embassies of different countries including India. He knows the art of wining and dining the decision makers. He is almost seventy years old and has started to re-evaluate his priorities. 'What to do with all that money?' He is talking about setting up a trust in India in his late father Sunder Singh Kohli's name to benefit bright young children, irrespective of their caste, religion or gender.

Nanak Singh Kohli was born in 1932, in a well-to-do family of Khukhrains in Pothohar near Rawalpindi, (now in Pakistan). The joint family of the Kohlis lived in a thirty-room haveli headed by Nanak Kohli's grandfather, the patriarch. Nanak was only eight years old when his mother Bibi Amar Kaur died, leaving behind young Nanak and his sister Kuldeep Kaur who was then twelve. Nanak's father remarried a year later.

'Our stepmother gave us so much love that my sister and I never missed our real mother,' says Nanak, and adds, 'You see our grandfather, the patriarch of the family was there to oversee everything, so our stepmother couldn't but treat us fairly.'

Nanak was fifteen when the family had to migrate to East Punjab in Independent India in 1947. The family had to rent a four-room apartment in Daryaganj. The Kohli family soon got used to living in crowded conditions. Nanak stayed in Simla for ten years, completed his Master's in Political Science, and started his first job as a lecturer in a college making Rs 180 a month. Nanak did not like his job. So he packed up and came to Delhi to study Law.

In 1959, Nanak's uncle's in-laws invited him to Patna to manage their Fiat Car Agency. His salary shot up from Rs 180 to Rs 1800. During this period Nanak got to know the bureaucracy—from the peon to the Chief Secretary and the Governor of the state of Bihar. Life in Patna was fun. Nanak was a member of the Bankipur Club. He played cards and dined with the 'elite' and was happy with his lifestyle. But Nanak was never happy staying in the same place with the same salary. He set up his own business—a finance agency. He was successful in his venture and started travelling to other parts of the country. In 1969 while he was visiting New Delhi, he met a very attractive young girl named Pammy who spoke good English. Nanak was mesmerized by her. He proposed to her and soon they were married.

He moved from Patna to Dehli to provide a proper social environment for his bride. Nanak asked his younger brother

Nanak and Pammy Kohli—a harmonious marriage of trade and poetry.

Pammy and Nanak Kohli's elder son Ranjit is married to a Hindu girl, Varnita.

Pammy and Nanak Kohli's lovely daughter Neka lives in Paris with her French husband, Julien.

Pammy and Nanak Kohli's youngest child Nishan is a very independent and private person.

to give up his job in the armed forces and help him set up his export business. Whatever he exported fetched such high returns that in 1978, he requested his wife Pammy to spend some time with relatives in Canada. While in Canada, Nanak thought of coming to Washington DC. He asked his wife Pammy if she could get admission in a good university. Pammy applied and got admitted in one of the top universities in America—Georgetown University. The tuition fee was exorbitant but that was no problem for Nanak. Since then, they have been in the Washington DC metropolitan area and prospering.

Pammy and Nanak have three children—a son Ranjit who is married to a Brahmin Hindu girl, a lovely daughter Neka who lives in Paris with her French husband, and their youngest child Nishan—a bright young bachelor who looks after the family business in New York.

I could not get much in terms of the nature of their international trade, but Nanak Kohli says that he represents over 50 American companies for his export business. He exports spare parts for defense equipment to India. He also represents American companies such as General Electric. Nanak has very close ties with the Embassy of India and does business with them on an ongoing basis.

It was no effort to interview Nanak's wife Pammy. At sixty she is still a lovely looking woman, a warm and liberated person. She has recently published a book of poems *Crying in the Wilderness* and continues to find self-expression in literary and artistic pursuits. She dotes on her two sons, her only daughter-in-law and her daughter. She has had an eventful life and was not hesitant to share it with me.

Pammy was born in Amritsar and was the sixth daughter of her parents. She felt she was an unwanted child (being a female and sixth in succession), but decided to show her parents that daughters too could bring honour and prestige to the family. But Pammy has always had an identity problem. Her parents ran a chain of military canteens and the family was so

Westernized that they had things unavailable to common Punjabis in India. She attended the best of schools and colleges. After obtaining her Bachelor's degree, she visited her elder sister and brother-in-law in England where they were posted as India's representatives. In England she studied Beauty Culture and became a society girl not only in London but also upon her return to India in New Delhi.

Things, however, did not turn out according to Pammy's expectations. She went to Georgetown University to get her Master's degree. She soon discovered that she was on her own. Nanak was travelling most of the time. She was left with her children and his money to contend with. Pammy tried to fill her loneliness with meaningful activities such as writing poetry and painting. She was too afraid to write explicitly about the romantic episodes in her life and turned to painting as an avenue for self-expression. The most fulfilling moment in her life was when her book *Crying in the Wilderness* was released in New Delhi.

Pammy feels that she has really blended well with the American way of life, while her husband keeps talking about returning to India to live a comfortable life in New Delhi. Pammy feels that she has found her niche in America. She is happy that her children have turned out to be such good individuals, in spite of the fact that Nanak was away most of the time.

I saw Pammy and Nanak last at Pammy's sixtieth birthday party. It was a real interfaith meeting. Ladies sang *Aarti—Om Jai Jagdeesh Hare* with candles all over. Bibi Amarjit Kaur sang Guru Nanak's *Gagan main thal,* then a Buddhist group sang some Japanese hymns. Pammy was wearing a cheerful looking Punjabi salwar kameez, and Nanak appeared in a Sikh turban.

Pammy and Nanak have similar views on Sikh leaders and Sikh affairs. They do not believe in parochialism and are opposed to the Khalistan movement. They are disappointed with the Sikh leaders. Nanak says, 'The problem is that every

Sikh is a leader and there are no followers.' Pammy and Nanak feel very unhappy about the role Sikh gurdwaras are playing in this country. Gurdwaras here are not places of worship, but platform for politics and power they feel. Pammy goes to the extent of saying that she feels much more comfortable going to a church than going to a gurdwara.

Nanak feels that Sikhs have a good future in India and abroad. Sikhs have the tenacity and courage, they are hard-working and they will beat any odds.

'What about *Rehat Maryada?*' I asked.

'I am clean-shaven, so are my sons, but I am a Sikh, that is good enough for me. It is too cumbersome to sport a beard and a turban. Sikhs waste too much time on these formalities. Instead of wasting time on applying hair fixers and tying *thathaas* and *pugris* they could engage in some useful activity.'

In Washington DC's elite circle, he is known as Mr Rolls Royce as he is one of the few to own one. He lives in a large mansion in the suburbs. Having started out with a salary of a mere Rs 180, he has gone on to become a multi-millionaire. He is also married to a lady who writes verse in English.

UNITED STATES OF AMERICA

The General Without an Army

DR GURMEET SINGH AULAKH

A general without an army would be an apt description for Dr Gurmeet Singh Aulakh who remains the sole upholder of Khalistan. While others have realized the folly of demanding a separate Sikh State, Aulakh continues to send out propaganda literature from his office in Washington DC.

For the past 16 years Dr Aulakh has been seen on the Capitol Hill lobbying for the 'Freedom of Khalistan' for the Sikhs of Punjab. Although most of the Sikh leaders living in the West now would like to see Indian Sikhs integrate with the mainstream Indians, Dr Aulakh is still fighting for a separate Sikh homeland. Here is the summary of an interview I conducted with Dr Aulakh in which he talks of his background, and expresses his views on Sikh affairs.

Dr Aulakh was born and brought up in Lyallpur (now in Faislabad in Pakistan). He received his early education in Amritsar and after getting his Bachelor's degree from Khalsa College Amritsar, worked in the same college in the Department of Agriculture until 1965 when he decided to migrate to the United Kingdom.

Gurmeet Singh Aulakh is the President of the Council of Khalistan.

Gurmeet Singh Aulakh being greeted by President Pervez Musharraf of Pakistan.

'Why did you decide to leave India?' I asked him.

'Curiousity,' he said in return. 'I wanted to see the world and get higher education.' He taught Science to High School students and worked towards getting a post-graduate degree in Teacher's Training from Jordan Hill College in Glasgow, Scotland. In 1970, he decided to migrate to the United States. He got his Master's degree from North Carolina University, then moved to Washington DC, to get a Ph.D. in Molecular Genetics from Howard University from where he graduated in 1973.

Dr Aulakh says his research was recognized by the international scientific community, and he was appointed a special expert at the National Institute of Health in the Laboratory of Oral Medicine. He is the author of over 25 scientific papers and chapters in books related to the field of recombinant DNA. In 1977, the proceedings of the National Academy of Sciences showed unequivocal evidence of the footprints of viral genetic material in human cancer tissue which was absent in the normal tissue of the same person. The discovery was made by Dr Aulakh in collaboration with Dr Robert Gallo of the National Cancer Institute.

After the Indian Army stormed the Golden Temple in 1984 his sense of betrayal was so strong that he left his distinguished position as a Research Scientist at Harvard University 'in order to fight for the rights of Sikhs'.

Dr Aulakh worked with Didar Singh Bains, General Jaswant Singh Bhullar and others to establish the World Sikh Organization (WSO) with its headquarters in Washington DC. He suspects that General Bhullar was planted by the Government of India to destroy the WSO.

'Bhullar did that by shifting its headquarters to Canada where it lost its visibility and impact.' He alleges that General Bhullar disappeared with all the WSO money, and was rewarded by the Government of India.

Dr Aulakh claims to have been appointed the President of

the Council of Khalistan by the Panthic Committee and the Sarbat Khalsa at Amritsar on 7 October 1987. As President of the Council of Khalistan Dr Aulakh says, 'I have the overwhelming task of refuting Indian Government's propaganda, which brands any politically active Sikh as a terrorist. I also bring to bear international pressure on the Indian Government to grant freedom to the Sikhs.'

'Are you in touch with the Indian Sikhs for whose freedom you are fighting?' I asked.

'Yes I am very much in touch with the masses in Punjab. I am also in touch with the Human Rights leaders in Punjab. Of course I have nothing to do with government cronies like Badal, Tohra and Maan,' he said. 'Those mercenaries are more interested in preserving their wealth than worrying about the destinies of the poor masses.'

I ventured to ask him the same question that Sardar Khushwant Singh usually asks most Khalistanis—to draw the map of Khalistan. Dr Aulakh had an answer ready, 'All Punjabi-speaking areas that have been fraudulently given to Haryana and Himachal Pradesh alongwith the present Punjab, will be our Khalistan.'

'So we will be surrounded by Pakistan and other neighbouring countries?' I was looking at him in disbelief.

'We will not be surrounded by these countries; we will have a common border with them. On the North will be Kashmir and on the South will be India. Look at Afghanistan, it is surrounded by Iran in the North and on the other side is Pakistan.'

He admires Indian Kashmiris who may not be more than seven million in number, but have been fighting the mighty Indian Government for the past fifty-six years. He became impatient while talking about the Sikhs. 'I don't know what is wrong with them, they are over 23 million. Why can't they fight for their freedom?'

'Do they want to fight?' I asked.

Dr Aulakh became angry, 'Two hundred fifty thousand having been killed since 1984, and over fifty-two thousand still in jails under TADA, don't you think they want to fight?' Dr Aulakh started to recount his achievements. 'I, alongwith another person have been lobbying the political leaders at Capitol Hill in Washington DC. Anything happening to the Sikhs in India is brought to the notice of the US Congress, and becomes a part of recorded history. We have internationalized the violations of human rights in India. On 25 June 1992 I helped secure a major victory for the Sikhs with the passing of the Burton Amendment to foreign aid package. The House of Representatives voted 219 to 200 to cut off 24 million dollars in US developmental aid to India in protest of India's violations of human rights against the Sikhs and Kashmiris.'

'Dr Aulakh, you know that you are a controversial figure even amongst the Sikhs because of your links with Pakistan and with the ISI,' I said casually.

'I am not a controversial figure. I am an honest dedicated person fighting for Sikh freedom. And all that gossip about my links with ISI is hogwash,' he replied.

'How much support do you have among the Sikhs of America?' I knew I had rattled him.

Dr Aulakh didn't even pause to think. 'This is the sixteenth year of my work—fighting for the Sikh movement. Ninety-five per cent support comes from the Sikhs living in the United States, the remaining five per cent comes from Sikhs living in other countries such as the United Kingdom, Canada, when I go to visit them. It is not my cause, it is their cause. I am only working for them. You know the saying, "Khalsa badshah or bagh (A khalsa is a king and a rebel)." ' He had fire in his eyes.

I tried to change the subject. I asked him if he knew about female feticide, especially in some areas of Punjab.

'Yes,' he said, 'I know the male-female ratio has gone down to 878 females per 1000 males in Punjab. This is to be condemned. And let me add here, all Sikh girls should become college graduates and should refuse to be forced into anything. My daughter, Avtinder Kaur was the eldest in the family. She is now the Vice President of Hilton Corporation in Washington DC.'

'Is your daughter married?' I asked.

'She was married, has two kids—a boy and a girl, but her husband was violent. She got rid of him. She gets no alimony. She doesn't need any.'

'How about your sons, are they Khalsas like their father?'

'My son Bikramjit Singh, the younger one, wears a turban, but trims his beard. The older one is clean-shaven. What can you do these days?'

'How did you stay attached to the Khalsa spirit? Did you have any problem getting your first job in England?' I asked.

'Not at all. Even in 1965, when there were just a few Sikhs in the Western world, I went around with my turban. In fact I was extremely successful as a teacher and no one questioned me.'

'What is you daily routine?' I wanted to wrap up the interview.

'I work for the cause of Khalistan 24 hours a day. I review newspapers. If there are stories about human rights violations anywhere in the world, I highlight them in our newsletter—17,00 letters going overseas, 8,000-9,000 to India. I disseminate information on Sikhism. I lobby politicians. And of course, I find time to play with my grandchildren. I am hard-working, and as sturdy as a rock. When you work hard, your body cooperates.'

UNITED KINGDOM

Holding Aloft the Khalsa Banner in Britain

DR KANWALJIT KAUR AND INDARJIT SINGH OBE

'It was a punch to the stomach that first established Indarjit Singh as a force to be reckoned with. He was at Primary School in Sutton Coldfield at the time. As a Sikh, he was in a minority of four, the other three being his brothers. Apart from having a skin colour different from 600 or so pupils, they wore turbans—not a common sight in the playgrounds of Middle England in the 1940s,' wrote Chris Arnot in *Life With the Lions.*

The story was of one particular tall bully who received his comeuppance when Indarjit lashed out at him.

'I caught him in the stomach because that's as far as I could reach,' he recalls. 'To my astonishment he went down. It was the first time I realized that I had a strong left arm. From then on, the other children were terrified of us and I had a sort of aura.'

The aura is still there. As the founder of the Network of Sikh Organizations, his influence has made him something of a touchstone for the British establishment. Prince Charles, bishops and the metropolitan police seek his views on problems, if any, of the Sikh community in Great Britain. Cabinet ministers accept his invitations to major festivals. BBC Radio 4 invites him to express his views on Today Programme's 'Thought for the Day'. He is a frequent contributor to the *Times, Guardian, Independent* and other newspapers and magazines. Not only is he a familiar face on 'Thought for the Day,' on Radio 4's Today Programme, but several TV documentaries have been made on him.

Indarjit is widely recognized as the voice of the British Sikh community. He edits the *Sikh Messenger.*

In 1989 Indarjit Singh became the first non-Christian to be awarded the Templeton Prize 'for the furtherance of spiritual and ethical understanding'. In 1991 he received the Interfaith Medallion for services to religious broadcasting, and was awarded the Order of the British Empire in June 1996.

Indarjit Singh was born in Amritsar in September 1932, the second son of Dr Diwan Singh, an outspoken supporter of the nationalist movement. After qualifying as a doctor, Dr Singh migrated to England with his wife and two sons and set up practice in Birmingham.

Indarjit and his three brothers were the only foreigners in their school. And since the four brothers with turbans had to constantly fight for survival, and they got good at it.

'It can really make you strong,' said Indarjit.

Indarjit graduated from college with a degree in Mining Engineering, and started looking for a job, 'but the turban was a hindrance,' he admits. 'I was looking for an excuse to go back to India.' In 1960 his parents and he returned to India, where he found a comfortable position in the coal mining industry at Asansol. Soon his parents started looking for a bride for him. They found Kanwaljit Kaur, the daughter of a prominent Sikh of Amritsar. Kanwaljit had just completed a Master's degree in History from Punjab University, Chandigarh. Within six months the couple were married, and Kanwaljit went to live with her engineer husband in Asansol.

Indarjit Singh OBE (left) with his wife Dr Kanwaljit Kaur and their two daughters (bottom) after being invested with the Order of the British Empire in June 1996.

Indar it Singh being felicitated by Queen Elizabeth II on being invested with the Order of the British Empire.

In 1960 the Punjabi Suba Movement was at its height. The government was doing its utmost to crush the movement.

'Sikhs were being given a raw deal,' said Indarjit. Under the assumed name V. Henry, Indarjit wrote articles in the newspapers as an Englishman, denouncing the discriminatory treatment meted out to the Sikhs. The media and the people responded to his viewpoint favourably.

Indarjit and Kanwaljit felt isolated in Asansol. So they decided to get together with their family in Amritsar and rethink their decision of staying on and working in India. In 1962, Indarjit and his younger brother decided to come back to England. His two daughters went to school in England. Today they are both doctors, married to Sikh doctors. Their children wear turbans like their grandfather.

Indarjit knows that anyone who is different in any way is subject to ridicule.

'If you value something, you won't throw it away,' he says. At home he educates these children about who they are; outside he works with civic bodies and the media. In 1999 he helped Prince Charles in drafting his speech at the tricentenary of the birth of Khalsa to admonish Sikh youth against seeking easy solutions to the problems of having to explain their heritage to others.

Since 1984 Indarjit has been publishing *Sikh Messenger* and has been writing articles about the Government of India. In 1998 Indarjit went to the United States, and in 1999 to India to produce programmes for the BBC. Six two-hour programmes were aired in 1999 marking the tricentenary of the birth of the Khalsa. Indarjit saw to it that Sikhism was included in the BBC Worldwide Service's Radio programmes, as one of the major religions of the world.

All through Indarjit was supported by his wife, Kanwaljit Kaur. When her younger daughter was still a toddler, Kanwaljit volunteered to help out in a nearby school. When one of her daughters became a doctor, and the other went to Cambridge to study Medicine, she decided to become a full-time teacher. She first became the Head Teacher, then Inspector of Schools.

In 1990, she completed her Ph.D. in Comparative Religions. Her thesis was entitled 'Contribution of Sikh Women to Sikh Society.' I saw tears in Kanwaljit's eyes when she talked about Mata Gujri. 'Were it not for her sacrifice, and the sacrifice of the two young sons of Guru Gobind Singh, we wouldn't be sitting here proudly talking about our glorious heritage.'

After the publication of Kanwaljit's Ph.D. thesis, publishers started sending her other authors' books to review. Since 1995 she has been publishing at least two books every year, and has written over a dozen books for children. Speeches that she has delivered at conferences have also been published.

Dr Kanwaljit has carved a niche for herself without being overawed by the growing influence of her husband. She is the Chairperson of the British Sikh Education Council, a consultant for schools' religious programmes on BBC Radio, a coordinator on National Committees for producing the National Syllabus on Sikhism and for bringing changes to legislation on collective worship.

When I met Dr Kaur in Gurdwara Shri Singh Sabha, Hounslow, she invited me to visit her in Guru Nanak Sikh School. There are about 240 students in this school, all Sikhs, but not all of them are practising Sikhs. There are about sixty per cent students who wear their long hair in *juras* or pigtails, the other forty per cent cut their hair.

'One of the students came to me and said, "I didn't want to cut my hair."

'Then what's the problem?' I asked. 'The eight-year-old boy said, "But my mother says if I don't cut my hair, who is going to comb it? Mother has to go to work early in the morning." '

'It is sad,' said Kanwaljit Kaur.

She explained that there were many such students whose

grandparents are devout Sikhs, but it is the parents, especially the young mothers, who saw things differently.

'May I join you in the assembly?' I asked.

'Yes, of course, if you have time.'

The students (almost 200) came and squatted on the floor, girls with dupattas covering their heads and boys with turbans or patkas. Even those whose hair was shorn, wore patkas. Dr Kaur talked to the students about routine matters of the school, then told them a story from Sikh history. The story was about the sons of Guru Gobind Singh, and asked them what they were willing to sacrifice as sons and daughters of Guru Gobind Singh.

Later as we discussed other Sikh issues, both Indarjit and Kanwaljit agreed that Khalistan was not something Sikhs had asked for.

'We are not separatists, we have been separated.'

Kanwaljit and her husband visit India almost every year. In 1999 they visited all the historical gurdwaras in India with their grandchildren.

UNITED KINGDOM

Member of British Parliament

PIARA SINGH KHABRA

At seventy-seven Piara Singh Khabra is seeking election to the House of Commons for the third term. He was first elected in 1992 from Ealing, Southall. Then he was with the Opposition Labour Party. Today he is with Tony Blair's Labour Government.

Khabra's success as a people's representative can be gauged from the fact that in 1992 he won with a margin of 7,000 votes. In 1997 he increased the margin to 22,000. Currently, he is a member of the Labour Party Departmental Committees for Foreign and Commonwealth Affairs, Home Affairs, International Development and Chairman of the All-Party Indo-British Group.

How did he get there? He is a Punjabi Jat Sikh from a village called Kaharpur in Hoshiarpur district. My host in London, Daya Singh Aulakh was not keen on meeting Khabra. 'He is a communist, not a Sikh,' said he. Daya Singh drove me to a community hall where several others, mostly Punjabis, were

Piara Singh Khabra, member of the British Parliament, with former Foreign Secretary, Robin Cook, and a friend.

Piara Singh Khabra, Member of the British Parliament, with Prime Minister Tony Blair, Deputy Prime Minister John Prescot and school children.

present. They were to discuss problems faced by members of their families in India waiting to come to England.

A frail looking elderly man in a suit and a tie walked in briskly. He looked around and asked his assistant, a six-foot tall, hefty looking South Indian, if the lady journalist had arrived.

'No, Sir, I didn't see any journalist come in?'

'But she had told me she would be here at 1.00 p.m. I am a little late.'

I stood up and introduced myself, and asked him for another appointment when I could talk to him undisturbed by others. The following day I met Mr Khabra in his office overlooking the Thames. His assistant, a young Englishman who was also sitting in the same office, was typing away. Every now and then he would pick up the phone, and announce, 'Piara, your 2 o'clock is here.'

Piara Singh told his assistant to have him wait. After about twenty minutes, there was another call, 'Piara, your 1 o'clock is still waiting, and now your 3 o'clock is here.'

We started talking in our Punjabi village dialect.

Born on 20 November 1921 Piara Singh Khabra was the youngest of four brothers and a sister, and was only eight years old when his father died. He went to Primary School in his village and had to walk several miles to go to High School in village Mahalpur.

'Often I walked barefoot as I had no shoes,' he said. 'But that did not deter me. I always wanted to compete and win. I played football and did well in studies.'

After completing High School, Piara Singh joined Government College in Hoshiarpur to study Political Science and Philosophy. War broke out in 1942, and he enrolled in the army. He served in the army for four years, then decided to come back to college to complete his education. After that he became a High School teacher.

One of his uncles who had migrated to Capetown returned

to his village. He had earned lots of money, built himself a house and bought more land. Hence his status in the village had risen. He was elected a member of the Panchayat, then as Sarpanch. This uncle was not educated and asked Piara Singh to take over as Sarpanch. Piara Singh was only twenty-two at the time. With this began his interest in village affairs. He became the Chairman of the Land Consolidation Committee, and helped villages out with the consolidation of their holdings.

Piara Singh renewed his membership in the All India Students Federation, and joined the Communist Party. The Government of Independent India was trying to strip tenants of their rights to own the land that they tilled. Piara Singh led an agitation on their behalf, and was arrested and jailed for six months. After his release, Piara Singh applied for admission to American universities. He was accepted by more than one university, but the American Embassy refused to grant him a visa because of his communist past. Instead he got a work permit and visa from the British High Commission.

'Obviously their intelligence in India was not as effective as that of the CIA,' said Piara Singh with a chuckle.

In 1959 Piara Singh Khabra, then thirty-five, arrived in London. The work experience in his bio-data was varied indeed. Factory work for a couple of years since his arrival in the United Kingdom from India; clerical work for three years with British Oxygen; Teacher for Inner London Education Authority for nearly fourteen years; Community worker for fourteen years.

Piara Singh went back to school and earned a diploma in Education from Whitelands College in London. He wanted to be a teacher. He was interviewed by several school authorities and told, 'You are not ready yet. English is not your mother tongue.'

Finally he found a job as a temporary substitute teacher going from one school to another. This experience helped him understand English children. He gained confidence, and finally found a full-time job in 1968. But with his bent of mind he was best cut out for a career in politics. He joined the Communist Party of Great Britain.

'I read modern books on Marxism, Leninism and read constitutions of different countries,' said Piara Singh.

One thing led to another. Four years later he joined the Labour Party. In 1978 he got himself elected as a Local Councillor and was appointed as Justice of Peace. During those years he got involved in community activities and held several offices such as Found Member and Treasurer of the Ealing Community Relations Council and Chairman of the Southall Community Law Centre. He was elected Education Secretary, then General Secretary of Indian Workers Association, Southall.

'We have a large number of ethnic people in this country. Our Indian/Pakistani people who had migrated to African countries such as Uganda and Kenya did not bother to participate in politics. My view is that if we are to stay here, and contribute as members to this society, why not take part in the politics of this country as well and become instrumental in the decision-making process?' said Piara Singh.

In 1992 Piara Singh won the Parliamentary election from Ealing, Southall. He won again in 1997 with a large margin. There were several reasons for Piara Singh's success.

'I was involved with workers' organizations. I was a magistrate. I always helped my constituents sort out problems relating, for instance, to education, employment, race relations, immigration.' I could see it for myself that he was accessible to everyone who came to see him.

Piara Singh was married to an Indian woman who bore him a son and died soon after. His son is a scientist living and working in Canada. Khabra then married a French Canadian woman named Beulah who had two daughters from the previous marriage. I could not meet Khabra's family, but I did notice their family picture on the wall of his office.

Piara Singh is now readying himself for a third term as Member of Parliament.

Though all his brothers and sisters are dead, Piara Singh keeps in touch with his village and the affairs of Punjab. In his opinion, 'The quality of leadership in Punjab is very poor. Education is very poor, character is lacking. Members of Parliament in India spent enormous amounts of money to win elections. Here in the United Kingdom my election expenditure never exceeded 9,000 pounds. While here we get elected to serve our community, out there in Punjab and in the rest of India, leaders expect people to come to them with garlands and honour them. All rubbish. Good people have a hard time, while corrupt people are shameless and amass wealth,' said Piara Singh.

Piara Singh has no time for Khalistan.

'I am dead against it. I even asked Dr Jagjit Singh Chauhan to tell me in what way we were different from Hindus, and why we want a separate state.'

He does not set much store by the Khalsa tradition of unshorn hair and beards either.

'Basic values are more important than the outward symbols,' he says. 'Any silly idiot can issue edicts from the Akal Takht. Who are they to tell us how we should live our lives? Religious leaders waste community money in corrupt practices. Instead, they should build schools, hospitals and roads.'

UNITED KINGDOM

Of Grit and Determination

GURDIP SINGH GUJRAL CBE

Meeting Gurdip Singh Gujral was an emotional experience. I asked him where he was born and educated. He told me that he was born in Chack 42 SB, Sargodha and that he went to school in Chack 29 SB in the Khalsa High School where my late father Sardar Jodh Singh had been the Headmaster.

Sixty-six-year-old Gurdip is now settled in London and is one of the richest Asians in England. His textile business has an annual turnover of 12 million pounds. He lives in a plush locality and drives an expensive car. He gives generously for charitable causes and is the Head of over half a dozen social organizations. Amongst others, he is the President of the International Punjabi Society, the Guru Gobind Singh Foundation (UK), the Nargis Dutt Society for Cancer Research and Relief, and the Chairman of the World Sikh University Senate, London.

Gurdip Singh is the sixth of the eleven children of Sardar Diwan Singh and Bibi Isher Kaur, who migrated from Sargodha in 1947 to settle in Sirasgarh village in Ambala. With limited means and close to a dozen children to feed and educate, Gurdip Singh's father could not afford to meet even the basic needs of his family. Gurdip Singh remembers how he had to walk three miles each day to go to school in village Mulana. After graduating with a B.Sc. from GMN College Ambala in 1953, he took up his first job on a monthly salary of Rs 100.

Gurdip Singh disliked working for others and wanted to start his own business. He worked on small jobs until 1965 when with a work permit in hand, he decided to migrate to the United Kingdom. He took up the job of sweeping floors in a factory. Another Indian who did a similar job took the broom from his hand and advised him to either go back to India or cut off his hair because he simply could not bear seeing a turbaned Sikh with a broom in his hands. Gurdip Singh did neither. He persevered. His wife got a job in a public office. So did Gurdip Singh. He was still not happy as he wanted to be his own master. He started selling brass trinkets and ethnic garments on the pavements at London's Petticoat Lane on weekends. After many years of standing in the bitter cold and rain he had saved enough money to start his own import business of ready-made garments in 1972. He now owns three warehouses and goes to India every two months to replenish his stocks.

Gurdip Singh is happy with what he has done with his life. He says that his best decision was to migrate to the United Kingdom, and his only regret is that he did not set up his own business earlier. He is very much aware of the growing competition from countries like China and Sri Lanka, but prefers to do business with Indian suppliers because that is still his motherland. The Punjab Government has recently honoured him with a Shiromani Award, Nishan-e-Khalsa at the celebration of the tricentenary of the birth of the Khalsa at Anandpur Sahib in Punjab.

Gurdip Singh has a younger brother and two sons working with him. His day starts at 4.30 a.m. when he gets up to

Hillary Clinton congratulating Gurdip Singh Gujral after he was appointed as a Commander of the Order of the British Empire (CBE).

Queen Elizabeth II conferring the CBE on Gurdip Singh Gujral.

accompany his wife to the gurdwara in Southall. Although his grandfather Lala Thakur Das was a Hindu and his father Sardar Diwan Singh the first in the clan to convert to Sikhism, he is proud to be a Sikh. Gurdip Singh has many relatives—an interesting mixture of Sardars and Monas (Hindus). He believes in giving to the needy but not to gurdwaras. He has donated handsomely towards medical research in cancer. In recognition of his services to the community, Gurdip Singh was made a Commander of the Order of the British Empire (CBE) in the New Year's honours list of 1998.

He is not in favour of Sikhs limiting themselves to Khalistan. He feels that Sikhs have a promising future worldwide.

UNITED KINGDOM

First Sikh Barrister in British Court

MOTA SINGH QC

Judge Mota Singh is the pride of Britain's Sikh community and is held in high esteem by mainstream Britons as well. He was the first Sikh Barrister to appear in British Court. His first appearance was in 1967 wearing a turban instead of the customary wig. Nobody raised an eyebrow. After his presentation the judge remarked, 'Mota Singh, it was a pleasure to listen to you. You represented your client very well. You are thorough.'

After eleven years of practising law, Barrister Mota Singh became Queen's Counsel. A year later he was made a part-time judge, and in three another years, in 1982, he was made a full time judge of the British Circuit Court.

Mota Singh remains a devout Sikh deeply involved in community affairs. He is on the Board of Trustees of the Windsor Leadership Trust headed by Field Marshal Lord Inge GCB DL. He is also a trustee of various religious, educational and charitable institutions.

Mota Singh was born in Kenya on 26 July 1930. He celebrated his fiftieth wedding anniversary with his wife

Mota Singh, Queen's Counsel (QC), the first Sikh barrister in the British Court (left) holds court while his wife Sardarni Swaran Kaur enjoys the moment (bottom).

Mota Singh QC with Sardar Manjit Singh, Jathedar of Sri Anandpur Sahib.

Sardarni Swaran Kaur in 2000. The couple have three children —a daughter and two sons and several grandchildren.

Mota Singh is the eldest of six children of Sardar Dalip Singh and Sardarni Hernam Kaur who had lived in Kenya since the beginning of the twentieth century. Mota Singh has four younger brothers and a sister, all highly educated, and well placed in their respective professions. Except for one brother who lives in Paris as an employee of Air India, they all live in or around London. Their mother Sardarni Hernam Kaur, who is eighty-six years old and widowed since the last fifty-five years, has keys to the homes of each one of her sons.

Mota Singh wanted to study Medicine. His plans changed while he was still in High School in Kenya. His father who owned a garage was killed while trying to save an Indian from a black African robber. Mota Singh was then sixteen years old. Sardarni Hernam Kaur was left with six children, Mota Singh being the oldest. The elders of the family decided to let him finish his High School education. After getting his High School diploma, Mota Singh took up a job as a clerk in the Police Department. Then he switched over to the Railways (still as a clerk) but also started studying for a D.Sc. in Economics as an external student. After that he joined Lincoln's Inn in Nairobi as a clerk and took the first part of the Bar examination in Nairobi.

Mota Singh was only seventeen years old when the parents of a girl put five shillings in his palm and said, 'This boy is ours.' And so it was. Mota Singh met his fiancée Swaran Kaur twice in the course of three years before they were married. 'Swaran and I grew up together,' says Mota Singh.

Mota Singh came to Great Britain to take his Bar examination and became a barrister in 1956. He went back to Kenya to become a practising advocate. Within a year he was elected as a city counsellor. At the age of thirty-one, he became Alderman of the City of Nairobi—the youngest ever member of the Counsel and Alderman.

In 1963 he left Kenya to come back to London. By that time he was the father of three children. He became an assistant legal advisor to one of the largest groups of property companies in the country. Within two months the company promoted him to a higher post. He had the confidence to ask his employers to release him to practice Law. The company promised enough business as their legal advisor to cover his existing salary and more.

Mota Singh became a successful and popular barrister. He had such a roaring practice that he started referring some of his cases to his English contemporaries. He was known as a brown Englishman among his contemporaries. He specialized in landlord and tenant cases. He always felt at home with the British contemporaries. The word 'discrimination' never crossed his mind. Within twenty-two years of becoming a barrister, Mota Singh was made Queen's Counsel. It took him only three more years to become a Judge in the British Circuit Court.

When Asians from Uganda were expelled by Idi Amin in the early 1970s, they arrived in England in thousands. Mota Singh was nominated to represent their case before the United Nations.

UNITED KINGDOM

Youngest Asian as Queen's Counsel

MANJIT SINGH GILL QC

Manjit Singh Gill migrated to England at the age of six. 'You must meet Manjit Singh Gill QC. He is the youngest Asian to have become Queen's Counsel at the age of thirty-nine,' said a friend in New York. Only leading members of the Bar are made Queen's Counsel. As QC Manjit leads a team of lawyers in courts and presents his side of every case. The previous and only practising Sikh to be made Queen's Counsel was Mota Singh, and that was more than twenty years ago.

In 1998 the Attorney General appointed Manjit Singh as one of a small handful of special advocates authorized to represent the interests of appellants before the Commission in national security cases. He has taken up many discrimination cases, and has often handled cases for the Commission for Racial Equality. He has spoken regularly at seminars, training sessions, and international conferences on various areas of practice, and has also appeared before United Nations Human Rights Committees.

In the 1980s he was involved in a number of initiatives

against race discrimination in the legal profession. In the mid 1990s he was involved in setting up the Discrimination Law Association. He has conducted some high profile terrorists' trials, for instance, the conspiracy to assassinate the Indian Prime Minister, Indira Gandhi. He is also the editor of Immigration and Nationality Reports. His chamber has a team of thirty-one barristers. It is the first truly multiracial barristers' chamber in the United Kingdom.

Manjit was only six years old when his parents migrated to the United Kingdom in 1966. Non-whites, Asians, and Africans were all called 'blacks'. They were the butt of ridicule. A boy wearing a turban or a jura would be asked if he had an apple under the towel wrapped around his head.

Manjit has an older brother and a sister. All three went to a Grammar School in Birmingham. They were the only students in their classes who belonged to an ethnic minority, and had to face discrimination individually. Manjit was good at games and played soccer for his school. He also learned to swim and would go around with his wet hair in a jura after swimming lessons. He was well liked by his schoolmates as he was good in sports and studies.

Manjit coped well with the challenges of belonging to an ethnic minority in his school and college. However, he kept his anger in check hoping one day he would win his crusade against injustice.

Manjit's father being an architect wanted him to follow in his footsteps professionally. Others suggested Medicine. But Manjit was set on studying Law, and eventually became a barrister. After getting his LL.B. (Hons.) degree from the university, Manjit had to do a year's apprenticeship with a law firm. That was not easy. It was even more difficult to persuade solicitors to have him argue cases in courts. He, however, overcame both the hurdles. The idea of being a tax lawyer advising big companies on how to avoid taxes did not grab his fancy. He was always interested in human rights issues. Now he has an international practice covering Human Rights Law, Public Law (especially community care, education, housing, immigration, local government, mental health, social security), European Law, employment, discrimination, property and crime.

Right from the start, Manjit had been involved with matters concerning human rights. In 1984 major events occurred in Punjab, and the ripple effect was felt worldwide. Manjit got involved with the aggrieved Sikh community living in the United Kingdom. He started spending more time in community affairs and also started handling more human rights cases. He handled cases that involved Sikhs seeking asylum, Muslim women's right to wear a headscarf, and Sikh men's right to wear the *kirpan*.

In 1985, Manjit was introduced to Kamaljit who was also pursuing Law. They liked each other, but took time to know one another before deciding to get married. They have two children—a daughter, Simran who is twelve and a son Adersh who is eight. Later we talked about Kamaljit's job as a lawyer with a private health care agency, and about Simran's arguments in school with other students and teachers about keeping long hair and observing Sikh traditions. I asked Manjit to give me an example of his work for human rights.

'I can think of one extreme case. There was a refugee from one of the Middle Eastern countries, who committed a crime in desperation. After having served his term in jail he was let out. He was sleeping on the streets, had no food, no shelter, no job. He was literally dying of starvation. I represented this case. The refugee was granted basic governmental assistance till he could find a job.'

Manjit continued, 'Then there were a number of people from war-torn countries such as Kosovo, who came to England as refugees. Two very prominent barristers were put up against me while I represented these victims, who had been shunted from one country to another, each refusing to accept them as refugees. I won the case. They were granted refugee status in Great Britain. Then there have been cases of Sikhs seeking refugee status. I know they would have been killed as soon as they had landed in Punjab,' said Manjit.

Manjit deplores caste distinctions among Sikhs.

'There are Jat gurdwaras, and Ramgarhia gurdwaras. We go to all of them, and try not to tie ourselves to any one denomination. Caste system matters in marriages. People try to stick to their own communities, but things are changing. Whether parents like it or not, there are going to be more and more intercaste marriages among Sikhs in this country,' he said.

He spelt out his views on Khalistan: 'Sikhs should decide if they want a separate state, and whether they can attain statehood without bloodshed. Ideally, the Government of India should have a dialogue with Sikh leaders, but if that does not work, the different factions of Sikhs should work together. At the moment there is peace and quiet, but things have not been resolved. Indian democracy should create safety valves to contain the resentment of minorities. The Indian state must adopt a different approach in dealing with minorities.'

Manjit Singh Gill QC has the singular distinction of being the youngest Asian to become the Queen's Counsel.

Reuben Singh (left) with his Midas touch, is an icon for Sikh youth in the United Kingdom.

UNITED KINGDOM

Schoolboy Millionaire

REUBEN SINGH

An article in a British business journal has a box item summing up Reuben Singh's career:

1976: Born on 20 September in Cheshire. Educated in William Hulme's Grammar School and Manchester Metropolitan University.

1995: Founded Miss Attitude.

1998: Sells Miss Attitude, becomes one of the government's Ambassadors for Entrepreneurship and is invited to sit on DTI's Competitiveness Council.

2000: Invited to sit on DTI's small-business council.

2001: Invited to sit on DCMS Government online advisory board.

Reuben Singh is quite flamboyant. He had a Bentley made for himself. Bright yellow colour, black leather seats, personalized number plate, walnut dashboard with a gold *khanda kirpan*—the emblem of the Khalsa. It costs Reuben £270,000. I got it last week,' he told his interviewer. 'It is the only one of its kind in the world.'

Reuben's parents owned a modest business in Delhi. In the 1960s his father was at Manchester University to do a Master's degree in Business Management. In the 1970s, his parents migrated to England to set up business in Manchester. Both their sons were born in England and sent to English schools. They were a close-knit family and orthodox Sikhs—no alcohol, no tobacco, and vegetarians. To start with, the only family friends were Lord and Lady Swaraj Paul.

Why the odd name Reuben? His parents wanted to give him the non-Sikh name Ruby. His Jewish neighbour suggested Reuben. So Reuben it was and still is.

The idea of setting up his own business came to him while he was still at school. He would accompany his mother on Saturday evenings as she went from shop to shop looking for different items like handbags, watches, pulses.

'Why not make these things available under a single roof?' he asked himself. Soon he opened a shop in Manchester's Arndale Centre. He named it Miss Attitude. It did well. So he opened another, then another, and a whole chain of Miss Attitudes. By 1999 he had 500 outlets with over 1000 employees. Then he sold the entire chain. Nobody knew how much he got for the deal. It is believed it was around 50 million pounds. He was only twenty-two at the time.

Reuben could have lived in style on the interest. But that was not good enough for him. And England was too small to contain his lofty ambition of becoming one of the richest people in the world. He spent six months in the United States exploring possibilities of different kinds of businesses he could enter, and has yet to make up his mind.

Meanwhile he has been back in India for a while and went to Amritsar to be baptized as a Khalsa. He admitted to his interviewer that he had three W's in his life: the first W is wealth—he's got that. The second W stands for women—there are plenty waiting to get close to him. The third W is for a wife. He is quite clear—his preference is an Asian, most likely a Sikh.

UNITED KINGDOM

Making Souls Meet

PIARA SINGH AULAKH

His first job in England was loading trucks. He qualified to become a teacher. Today he is the leader of his community in Hounslow, and has given it a new Sikh gurdwara and school. His wife and he run a matrimonial agency to help young Sikhs to find life partners from within their own community.

After bowing to the *Guru Granth Sahib* in the Gurdwara Singh Sabha in Hounslow, we walked down to the office on the ground floor. A tall, slender, middle-aged sardar stood up as did everyone else. '*Aao Chachajee* (Please come in, Uncle),' he addressed Daya Singh Aulakh (my host in London who had arranged for me to meet the prominent Sikhs in London) before greeting me.

'I have arranged appointments with members of the community in the London area. You will meet them in a room set aside for you,' he said to me.

My first interview was after lunch. I sat down and looked around the room and at the men and women assembled there.

Piara Singh occupied the Chairman's seat. He handed over

a printed leaflet to a lady who wanted to host a langar at the gurdwara. He invited the next lady in the line to tell him about her project. It was all very informal and businesslike. I picked up a magazine full of pictures of Queen Elizabeth II and the Prince of Wales with leaders of the Sikh community. I read Prince Charles' address at the tricentenary of the birth of the Khalsa:

'I have come to know your community over many years both in Britain and in India and we remember visiting Amritsar back in 1980. In fact I have particular memories of that occasion when a very large crowd of friendly and welcoming Sikhs carried me bodily off my feet around the entire site of the Golden Temple.'

There were pictures of Prince Charles playing polo with Sikh in their turbans. The address continued:

'So my admiration for Sikhs grew by leaps and bounds. I have also developed a great respect and admiration for your faith. Sikhism teaches and Sikhs aspire to tolerance, a willingness to stand up and be counted, a repudiation of discrimination on grounds of caste and race, the dignity of women and the ideal of the saintly soldier. These values have, I think, a universal appeal.'

There were more tributes paid by the royalty to the Sikhs assembled for the occasion at the Royal Albert Hall. The last sentence was significant:

'So I would urge you not to caste away your unique heritage and traditions in response to the siren voices of modernity.'

There was a wedding in the gurdwara, and the groom happened to be a *gora*. Piara Singh prepared me for the shock. 'The bride comes from a prominent Sikh family. She could have married any Sikh boy the liked, but it is a matter of hearts. She is in love with this gora, so what can you do? We have to yield to our children!'

Suddenly, I ran into a woman I had often met at the Guru Nanak Foundation in Maryland, in the United States.

Piara Singh Aulakh watches as the *Guru Granth Sahib* is carried in a procession to the gurdwara.

Piara Singh Aulakh with other distinguished elders.

'What are you doing here?' she asked. This lady, Mrs Reddick, is married to a Christian but retains her Sikh identity. Her daughters conduct Sikh Youth Programmes at the Guru Nanak Foundation Gurdwara in Maryland.

In the langar hall, there were about fifty children. Most of them were whites, while the rest were Indians and Pakistanis. They had their heads covered with yellow scarves, and their teacher, a white Englishman, was instructing them on how to eat Indian roti and *daal!* I was intrigued.

'What are they doing here?' I asked.

'They have come to visit our gurdwara in connection with a class on multiculturalism. They have come here to find out how the Sikhs worship and break bread together,' said Piara Singh.

Langar is served throughout the day. People walked in late in the afternoon, to be served by volunteers, mostly elderly men and women, who prefer being with others to sitting around doing nothing.

We returned to the office to get down to interview one of the dozen Sikhs lined up for me. I finished one and felt too tired to go on. Before I could retire, an elderly woman accosted me. 'Are you here for a *rishta?*' she asked me.

'What rishta?' I asked.

'I mean are you looking for a match for one of your children?'

'What makes you think that?' I asked, amazed at her audacity.

'Don't get offended. I am here to look for a match for my granddaughter, who is a medical doctor, but hasn't found a husband on her own. These people, Piara Singh Aulakh and his associates run a matrimonial service for Sikh families.'

Piara Singh walked in. While he went over a list of probable matches for educated Sikh females with this woman, sitting at a distance, I could hear her say, 'I called you and told you that I am looking for a Jat boy, preferably clean-shaven. She may agree to meet a turbaned Sikh, but my first condition is that he has to be a Jat.'

I don't know what transpired in the end. It was around 6 p.m. when Piara Singh and I left the gurdwara to meet the other Aulakh in his home. As we walked down the streets of Hounslow, I saw many turbaned Sikhs and felt strangely comfortable.

'The pugri is a plus point and I can say that from my own experience,' said Piara Singh. 'But my older son took it off to marry a Hindu girl.' In Piara Singh's home three ladies, his wife Harbir and two daughters-in-law were busy getting dinner ready. Children were playing in the backyard. Daya Singh and Gursharan arrived soon after. Dinner was laid out and we all sat down to eat. Daya Singh was served first, then we helped ourselves. As soon as we picked up our forks and spoons, Jiwan stopped us. 'Uncle is praying.' I saw Daya Singh sitting with his hands folded over his plateful of rice, daal, yoghurt, and vegetables. Finally Daya Singh opened his eyes and motioned everyone to start.

After a hearty meal, we came into the living room. Piara Singh turned on the TV and pulled out a video cassette which he asked us to watch. It was of a reception thrown by the Hinduja brothers. Political leaders including Prime Minister Tony Blair, and India's Who's Who were seen shaking hands with the Hinduja brothers. Piara Singh was amongst them. I had not thought of interviewing Piara Singh till I saw the video.

Piara Singh Aulakh is the oldest of six children of Charan Singh and Mohinder Kaur. He was born and brought up in village Aulakh. He received his primary education in his village before going on to join the National Sikh College in Sathiala (near Baba Bakala). He graduated with a Bachelor's degree in Mathematics A and B course, in 1960. In 1961, he did his B.Ed. from Lyallpur Khalsa College, Jalandhar and joined the Punjab Government Service as a teacher. In 1965, at the age of twenty-six he got a visa to migrate to the United Kingdom.

When he arrived in London his friends and relatives warned him that he would find it hard to get a job in England unless he cut off his hair and beard. Piara Singh disregarded their advice and proceeded on his own, from door to door looking for a job and finally he landed one as a loader. It was a back-breaking job. Seeing him work without complaining for one and a half years, his employer decided to give him a raise.

'He made me in charge of a division, gave me an office, a telephone and an assistant. I was very happy. I was my own boss now,' said Piara Singh. A year later he was able to get a teaching position at a British school. His wife Harbir whom he married a week before leaving for the United Kingdom turned out to be an ideal companion. 'We are happy together,' says Piara Singh. The diamonds in Harbir's nose and ears flashed as she turned her face the other way, blushing up to her ears.

Piara Singh and Harbir have two sons—Satkamal Singh and Harkamal Singh. Both are computer analysts and have well-paid jobs. The younger one, Harkamal Singh settled for an arranged marriage with a young Sikh girl, while the older one—Satkamal, married a Hindu girl who he had met at college. He shaved his hair, and took off his turban while he was away from home going to college at Nottingham University. The father was deeply hurt but decided to swallow his pride, and accepted Satkamal and his Hindu wife.

Piara Singh was able to help his parents migrate to the United Kingdom. They in turn brought their remaining two sons to England. Now, says Piara Singh, they have two sisters living in Punjab. The rest of the family is in London, and doing well. Piara Singh feels gratified that he was able to help his parents financially, and his siblings get an education that would ensure a better future for themselves and their children.

While Piara Singh had a good job as a teacher, his real satisfaction in life came from his involvement in community affairs.

'Until 1978 there was only one gurdwara in this area, in

Southall. We used to visit Southall every Sunday to go to the gurdwara and to see an Indian movie.' Then Piara Singh got the Sikhs of Hounslow to start weekly religious services in a rented hall in a school. The Sikh families would take turns to prepare langar (at home) which they brought to the school. This lasted for about two years.

'This could not go on forever,' said Piara Singh. 'We wanted to have our own gurdwara. The number of our members was increasing.'

Piara Singh and a few more Sikh families started pooling in their resources. They collected enough funds to buy two 'scouting huts'. They started using one of those huts as a gurdwara and the other for langar.

'We wanted to build our gurdwara. The building we are sitting in now was especially planned by an architect. A langar hall and offices on the ground floor, and the main prayer hall and classrooms on the upper levels,' said Piara Singh. Aulakh was proud to tell me that the Hounslow Gurdwara building was designed and constructed to meet the needs of the Sikh community and in keeping with the gurdwara traditions and architecture, whereas the other local gurdwaras were bought as ready-made structures from old churches and some department stores.

'We needed a sizeable loan from a bank to buy additional land, then construct the building we had envisioned,' said Piara Singh. 'No bank was willing to give such a huge loan without sufficient collateral. Then someone from amongst the bank officials suggested that a few of us could mortgage our homes to provide necessary assurance.' So Piara Singh and two other trustees—Jagjivan Singh and Ranjit Singh temporarily gave their homes to the bank to get a loan which they paid back in less than two years. They bought three more properties in the neighbourhood, demolished them and made space for the elegant building which now stands in the heart of Hounslow city.

'It took us twelve years to complete the project. The building was inaugurated in 1992. In the beginning we didn't have enough money to pay the *sewadars* and *granthis*—but now the building that cost us about 1.8 million pounds is worth 10–12 million pounds. We are never short of money for any of our gurdwara activities.'

Piara Singh gave an account of the gurdwaras.

'A Punjabi school was built, where 400 children between the age group of six and eighteen years are taught Gurmukhi. The teachers are funded by the local education authority.

'There was a great demand for learning kirtan. Darshan Singh teaches kirtan to adults and Rajeswari Kaur gives lessons to children. There is talk abut starting a separate music school in London for teaching Gurbani kirtan to all age groups. Children who learn kirtan in school, conduct programmes after the main diwan is over. They perform kirtan, do *ardas* and read vaak from the *Guru Granth Sahib.* And once a year these children conduct the main gurdwara programme including announcements from the stage.

'There is an increasing demand for English classes for adults because of the Sikh migration from Kabul. Even our own ladies who have come from Punjab are learning spoken English. Some college graduates from Punjab have to brush up their spoken English with the help of our teachers.

'Once a year, the *sangat* conducts a charity walk, and is able to raise £50,000–60,000 for the charitable activities of the gurdwara.

'Summer camps for Sikh youth are also held in the gurdwara premises.'

Piara Singh and Mohinder Singh Mand have been instrumental in starting matrimonial services for Sikhs. The services have been expanded to cover the whole of England and Scotland. This agency has proved to be so successful that Sikhs from Canada, the United States, Australia and South Africa register their sons and daughters of marriageable age out here.

Every issue of the gurdwara magazine *Gobind Marg* carries over 200 names of Sikh boys seeking life partners through the matrimonial services of the Hounslow Gurdwara. The magazine is sent free of cost to families that register their children names for suitable partners.

Piara Singh feels very proud that he has been instrumental in the growth and development of the Sikh community. He is a contented man, and looks forward to early retirement from his job as a teacher, so he could devote all his time to community service.

Piara Singh is not in favour of Khalistan. Although he was deeply hurt during the 'Operation Bluestar' and the genocide of Sikhs following the assassination of Mrs Indira Gandhi, he vents his anger on the government of those times. He has a very poor opinion of Sikh leaders because they do not consult the educated Sikhs on matters concerning the community.

Piara Singh is unhappy with the Sikh leaders of Punjab. He says, 'We have never invited any of them to our gurdwara even when they have been in town for so-called "missions" such as community service or *dharma prachar*. These leaders are divided among themselves and in 1999 at the tricentenary of the birth of the Khalsa, Badal and Tohra made a laughing stock of themselves in the eyes of the world.'

CANADA

Champion Wrestler

TIGERJIT SINGH

A wrestler was perhaps the last person on my list when I went to Toronto to interview a select group of Sikhs who had made Canada their home. My host drove me to this 100 acre estate outside Toronto.

We were met by the father and son team Tigerjit Singh and Tiger Ali Singh–in the sprawling lawn of their castle-like home. Mrs Sukhjit Kaur Hans, Tigerjit Singh's stunningly beautiful wife ushered us to their basement reception room. We were taken to their TV room, and shown a documentary film made by this Punjabi wrestler's family.

The focus was on Tiger Ali Singh, the twenty-six-year-old son of Tigerjit Singh who is one of the star performers of the World Wrestling Federation (WWF). Tiger Ali Singh was voted the most recognized Asian in sports entertainment in a recent Internet survey. He has been approached by Hollywood with roles that he has decided to not take on. Ford is already paying him big bucks for the commercials he has been doing for them in which he drives their new vehicle(s) every year.

I was overwhelmed. I wanted to talk to a person who came

from Punjab and had made it possible for his son to achieve fame as a *pehelwan*.

I found myself seated next to the fifty-six-year-old Jagjit Singh, now known as Tigerjit Singh in the Western world. He is six feet two inches tall, powerfully built and wears a *kurta pajama* and Patiala *jootee* embroidered with gold and silk. Born on 3 April 1944 in the village Dodra near Ludhiana, he was the fourth child of his father Major Gurbachan Singh who migrated to Canada after retiring in 1960.

Although educated, the children could not speak English, and jobs were hard to come by. The boys were robust. They played all day long, did weight-lifting and build their muscles. One day, they switched on the TV and the sixteen-year-old Jagjit (now Tigerjit) watched a wrestling match. 'I can do that!' he said to his father. Arrangements were made for him to meet a wrestling coach in Vancouver BC. The coach accepted him and taught him techniques of all-in wrestling.

He landed a contract for $100 per week for five years, which was good enough for him. Then an Australian coach took him to Australia for three months, from where he was taken to Japan, the Mecca of wrestlers. When Jagjit returned to Canada, his coach nicknamed him 'Tiger', which is how he became 'Tigerjit'.

Tigerjit Singh returned to Punjab in 1969. His parents arranged a meeting with Sukhjit Kaur Hans, the daughter of a police officer, and also an athlete and a college student. They liked each other and got married in 1970. Tigerjit Singh stayed in Punjab for some time and started coaching a team of wrestlers. He took Dara Singh on and defeated him. Eventually having blown up all his savings, he returned to Toronto with his pregnant wife.

In 1971 Tigerjit Singh was signed up to fight a Muslim wrestler. In a packed auditorium Tigerjit Singh took no more than three minutes to knock down his adversary. He won a cheque for $6,700.

Tigerjit Singh bought a new car. Since then he has never

Tigerjit Singh believes in training his brood young.

Tigerjit Singh in a particularly jubilant mood, with Vince McMahon of the World Wrestling Federation (WWF).

Tigerjit Singh, the champion wrestler being felicitated at a function by politician and film actor Raj Babbar and others.

looked back and has earned millions from his wrestling matches.

Tigerjit Singh reigned over the all-in wrestling world in Japan for over twenty-two years. He had to leave his wife and children behind in Canada for three months every year.

'I became the Hari Singh Nalwa in Japan!' said Tigerjit Singh with a sparkle in his eye. 'I did some crazy things like slapping a female film star who made fun of my turban... but that also meant that I made the headlines and my promoters were doubly protective of me, because I was the crazy Indian, the wired Punjabi.'

At one time Tigerjit Singh had 38 stitches on his body, and most of his bones which broke during wrestling matches, have been replaced by steel rods.

'The injuries I sustain from wrestling matches always heal miraculously,' he said.

After a while I switched over to Tigerjit Singh's son, Tiger Ali Singh, a name given to him by a family friend—the great Mohammed Ali. His real name is Gurjeet Singh and he is the eldest of the three brothers—the other two are Baldeep and Kulbir.

'My father was like Hulk Hogan and growing up under his shadow was not easy, but he was gone for three months a year and our mother did everything to send us to the best schools, play with us, help us with our homework, and never let us feel bored, never let us feel discriminated against. She was such a source of strength and comfort when there was open racism in our schools,' said Tiger Ali.

It was strange to see a big man with tears in his eyes. 'I always get emotional while talking about my mother. She is the real strength behind my father's successes. In fact, she is stronger than he is.' Then Tiger Ali calmed down and started relating his story.

He had won a scholarship to go to Notre Dame University and be in the university's basketball team. But before he could join college, he broke his ankle in an accident and the scholarship was withdrawn. Tiger Ali's dream was shattered. His father took him under his wing and tried to teach him the truth about life.

He took his first-born son to Japan for three months to teach him wrestling. Tiger Ali was simply dazzled by his father's popularity.

'He was like Michael Jackson,' said Tiger Ali. 'Can you imagine 60,000 people watching my dad win and chant "Shing, Shing, Shing..." The Japanese cannot pronounce "Tiger" very well, nor can they say "Singh". They could only shout "Shing" instead of "Singh". In fact the best way to counteract racism and bullying in school is to hit back. I did well in my studies as well as in sports. My brothers are both academically inclined and have graduated with college degrees in finance and management. They both have their own businesses,' added Tiger Ali.

'How did you manage to become such a big star in the wrestling world at such a young age?' I asked.

'Destiny, I think! Vince McMahon, the owner of WWF was looking for an Asian Hulk Hogan. I fitted the bill. He picked me up because of my ethic background and my ancestry,' he said looking at his father who was talking to Gurdeep Singh Saluja (my host in Toronto) while I interviewed Tiger Ali. He went on to explain, 'WWF TV is watched in more than 170 countries by 1.3 billion viewers each week. And these viewers voted me in as the most popular person to hate (I suppose Caucasian audiences find me offending) and the most recognized Asian in sports and entertainment.'

Soon there were threats to kill him alongside offers from Hollywood. WWF took Tiger Ali temporarily off the roster. The Toronto police mounted a helicopter vigil of the Singhs' estate.

The Singhs rarely go out. Tigerjit Singh trains his son Tiger Ali. They jog, do push-ups and swim in their pool.

All three of Tigerjit Singh's son have married girls of their parents' choice (from Sikh families) and live under the same roof with the patriarch Tigerjit Singh. They realize that the world outside can be hostile sometimes, and prefer to keep a low profile. Tigerjit Singh and his wife, both in their fifties, have started going to India at least once a year. There they are very warmly welcomed at *samagams* and kirtans. Tigerjit Singh believes in the Naamdhari's Guru and addresses him as *Satguruji.*

Two years ago Tigerjit Singh became the first ever wrestler to be made a United Nations Goodwill Ambassador. He wants to build hospitals in rural areas of Punjab, and donate as much as it takes to build the necessary infrastructure to make healthcare accessible to all Punjabis.

Tiger Ali however is concerned about the Punjabi youth. 'We need to give them hope,' he said. 'Our Punjabi youth is plagued with drugs and alcohol. We need to build fitness centres all over Punjab so that our youth can walk into a fitness centre (free of cost) rather than visit bars and drug dealers.'

Sukhjit Kaur Hans—Mrs Tigerjit Singh with rosy pink cheeks said, 'My husband may be a tiger outside, but at home he is the most loving husband and father.'

'Does it bother you that his profession is based on violence?' I asked.

'It bothered me a lot when he came home with broken bones and open wounds. I begged him to leave this profession but he had an answer to everything. He said, "I also inflict injuries on my opponents. These wounds heal and I like a good fight." Then I realized that my husband was not going to turn his back on wrestling, so I decided to support him.'

Sukhjit has never worked outside her home and does not miss doing so. Motherhood was a full-time job, while her husband travelled to Japan and other countries. Now she is a grandmother of three, and also has a gurdwara at home. She reads the scriptures daily and wants to teach Gurmukhi to her grandchildren so that they can learn to read from the *Guru Granth Sahib.* She is happy that her husband has finally retired from wrestling, and that they can spend time together at their estate with their brood.

CANADA

Sikh in Canadian Parliament

GURBAX SINGH MALHI

Starting out from a hamlet in the Moga district, Gurbax Singh Malhi went on to became not only the first bearded and turbaned Sikh Member of the Canadian Parliament, but also the first Member of Parliament of his kind in the Western world. Initially elected to the Canadian House of Commons in 1993, he was re-elected in 1997, and in the 2000 general elections.

Born on 12 October 1949 in a small village near Moga, he was the youngest of six siblings. He completed his elementary school education in his village, then walked three kilometres to attend Middle School in a neighbouring town. He was only five years old when his father died; his mother took charge of the children's education and the family's land and property.

Gurbax Singh Malhi was initiated into politics way back in childhood when his mother took him around canvassing for certain candidates for elections to the local Panchayat. After leaving Punjab, Malhi's father went to the United States in 1920, where he spent fifteen years in Fresno (California) working as a farm labourer. He returned to India with a lot of money

Prime Minister Jean Chretien holds up the *kandha,* the Sikh symbol which was presented to him by Gurbax Singh Malhi at the release of a stamp commemorating 100 years of Sikhism in Canada on 19 April 1999, in Hull, Quebec.

Gurbax Singh Malhi greets H.S. Brar at an official gathering while Prime Minister Jean Chretien looks on.

to get married and settle down in his ancestral village. This youngest child, Gurbax actively participated in the Panchayat elections. Politics got into his blood, '*Mainu tharak pai giya* (I fell in love with politics),' he said.

Gurbax Singh did his Bachelor's degree from Punjab University, and was into the second years of a Degree in Law at Agra University, when he met a young lady named Devinder Kaur who was visiting her parents in Punjab after a stay of three years in Canada. She had come home to get married, then take her future husband back to Canada. Gurbax Singh turned out to be the lucky man.

In April 1975 Gurbax and Devinder found themselves living in Canada, both doing odd jobs in factories. Devinder's job was more stable, and she never gave it up even after her husband became a Member of Parliament. She says, 'My time passes quickly when I am in the factory. I also meet my friends at work.'

The Malhis have two grown-up children—Gurinder Singh, their son and Harinder Kaur, their daughter. They are both in college. Gurinder wants to go into business. Harinder is studying Political Science and Law. Neither are keen to marry, but, 'If and when they do, they will marry within our community.' So their parents hope.

Gurbax Singh worked as a security guard, drove a taxi and even worked as a hard labourer before he moved into real estate in 1985. In seven years, he saved enough money to fight an election. Till then he had been canvassing for candidates of Indian origin to get elected for public office. None of them had succeeded. Then he ran for Local President of the Liberal Party, and was elected. In 1993 he won the nomination to the Canadian Parliament and was the first turbaned Sikh to became Member of the Canadian Parliament. Four other Sikhs opposed his election. Malhi even offered to step down if the sangat in the gurdwara so desired. They failed to reach an agreement. Malhi won his subsequent elections with even wider margins.

The secret of his success lies in his persistent efforts to work on issues affecting his constituents, and his ability to keep in touch with them on a personal level.

'I receive, on an average, fifty to sixty letters a day in my Ottawa office. Every Friday I meet hundreds of constituents in my local office,' said Malhi while undoing the knot of the bow tie he had been wearing since morning when he had attended three weddings in a row in different gurdwaras. He also visits his constituents of non-Indian origin, and works for their causes with equal zeal. For instance, each year he helps between eight to ten families from multicultural backgrounds—mainly Hispanics, in obtaining immigration papers and Canadian citizenship. More recently, he got the Right of Landing Fee ($975) scrapped.

Gurbax Singh seems to look for, or even create opportunities to be with his constituents. He organizes an annual summer picnic for them, an Akhand Paath and kirtan on New Year's Day at which more than 6,000 Indians are present. Last year, he organized a Diwali reception where Prime Minister Jean Chretien was the chief guest. However, the event that Malhi enjoys the most is Baisakhi on Parliament Hill. For the past eight years he has been organizing an Akhand Paath in his Ottawa office followed by a big celebration on Parliament Hill. Till date, the Prime Minister has not missed attending Baisakhi.

'Celebrating the birth of the Khalsa at Parliament Hill makes me feel so proud, and the media coverage we get is unbelievable,' he adds with a gleam in his eyes.

As an elected member of public office, he feels it is his duty to champion the cause of every person in his constituency. Late in 1999, he spoke in the House of Commons, supporting the right of a fellow Sikh, Pardeep Nagra, who was refused entry in the National Boxing Competition, because he sports a beard:

'Mr Speaker Sir, a great injustice has occurred in this great nation of ours, which traditionally values the principle of freedom of religion. Pardeep Nagra, a bright young man deeply involved in many community associations in my riding, has had his liberties suppressed...

'Mr Speaker, I request that the Minister for Amateur Sports withhold any funding to the Canadian Amateur Boxing Association immediately, as it is an association whose rules are contrary to Canada's fundamental freedom. . .

His speech did not go unheard. Nagra was permitted to box with his beard intact.

Gurbax Singh follows a strict routine of work, worship and exercise. He rises before 6 a.m., reads the morning prayer, the Japji, and exercises. 'I am a member of health clubs in Toronto and in Ottawa,' he avers.

'What do you think is your greatest achievement?' I asked him.

'I feel I have achieved something very great for the community when I sit in the House of Commons. I have made people aware of a people called Sikhs. When I won the election as an MP, no one was allowed in the House of Commons with a cover on his/her head. At the opening of the House, there used to be a prayer in the name of Jesus Christ. I talked to the Speaker of the House and got the prayer changed to a minute of silence so that non-Christians could also participate. 19 January 1994 was my first day in the House. It also happened to be Guru Gobind Singh's birthday. I asked the speaker of the House if I could speak for two minutes on the life of our Guru. That speech is still the best speech I have delivered. I often watch the recording of that speech on video-tape, and wonder how that great Guru empowered me at that moment.'

Gubax Singh has pronounced views on what Indian politicians could learn from the West. He says, 'The prevailing level of corruption cannot be put down to a single individual. I want to invite Indian politicians to come and see for themselves how a public servant should behave. Once an Indian politician asked me if I was coming with my bodyguards and a driver. I told him, I had no bodyguard, drove my own car, cut the grass and mowed the lawn in front of my house; I washed dishes after every meal and I shovelled snow from my driveway before I went anywhere during winter.'

Gurbax Singh is a fulfilled man. He said, 'When I stood for election in 1993, a fellow Sikh had told me that a turbaned Sikh is not likely to win an election even in a hundred years. I had replied, "If the Guru wants me to perform the duty of His servant in the House of Commons, he will make a way!" s

'My name is Gurbax, it should be spelled Guru-Bakshish—the Guru's gift.'

CANADA

The Right Deal

NAV AND ARVINDER BHATIA

It was a mild summer day, when Gurdeep Singh Saluja (see Introduction), drove into a sprawling complex packed with multicoloured cars glistening in the bright sunshine, and balloons reaching out to the vast blue sky.

'This is the dealership of Nav Bhatia. He is the only Indian in this country who owns a dealership in new cars,' said Gurdeep with a sense of pride. He drove around the whole complex in search of an appropriate place to park his car. We walked into an elegant, impeccably clean office. A smartly dressed young man met us at the reception.

'We have an appointment with Nav Bhatia, but we haven't come here to buy a car,' I said. I was eager to meet Nav Bhatia who is a familiar face on Canadian television and a household name for Indians in Canada.

We were ushered into the waiting room where we had a cup of coffee while talking to the man in charge of the service area. He had been with Nav for fifteen years and had won a national award for The Man of the Year in Hyundai Car Company, Canada.

Nav Bhatia walked in. He took us to his office, which was bustling with activity: phone calls, employees walking in and out with papers to be signed, messages to be dealt with, and newspaper clippings from the day's papers in which Nav had been mentioned along with other celebrities. We decided to head for Nav's residence. On our way out, Nav took us around his office and introduced us to his employees. Most of them had been working for him for over ten years; some travelled long distances to come to work.

'We started our export division in 1994. We provide cars to the rich and famous throughout the world. My best customer is King Hussein of Jordan,' said Nav as he opened the files of some new orders from overseas. Nav has over forty employees, including his elder brother who looks after the public relations department.

Nav's wife Arvinder keeps a beautiful home. Besides taking care of her husband, she looks after her daughter and her mother-in-law.

They also have a Indian servant who has been with the family since their days in Delhi. A few years into their stay in Canada, they arranged for the servant to come across, and are taking care of his children's education in India. Without wasting much time, I got down to my questions and asked him the secret of his success. He replied, 'I like people, I communicate well, and am not afraid to make new friends.'

Nav is the youngest of the four sons of Sardarni Shushil Kaur and Sardar Kalyan Singh Bhatia of New Delhi. The family was well off—they had an eyeglass factory and a sizeable outlet in South Delhi. Nav's brothers joined the family business. Nav went off to the United States to study Mechanical Engineering at the University of California. After completing his degree, he returned home to Green Park, New Delhi, got married to Arvinder, whom he had met at Gurdwara Rakab Ganj. Their parents had arranged the meeting.

Nav never wanted his wife to work outside his home and

Nav Bhatia readies to throw the basketball to start a game for the Raptors Basketball Team.

Nav Bharia in the company of Herb Dhaliwal, T-Sher Singh and Garry Sandhu (right to left).

made it clear to Arvinder that if she wanted to marry him, she would have to resign from her job at Escorts, where she had worked as the Executive Secretary. She did exactly that and hasn't looked back. Nav does not like to eat out, and comes home to eat his wife's home-cooked Indian meals. After serving lunch to her husband, Arvinder gets ready for her eleven-year-old daughter to come home.

Arvinder explained that she likes to spend most of the day with her daughter. 'I want her to depend on me as much as possible. This will keep her emotionally tied to her family and I know she will think twice before she does anything wrong.'

'Your family had such a successful business in India. What made you decide to migrate to Canada?' I asked Nav.

'My family had seen so much bloodshed in 1947, that we thought Delhi would be our permanent home. But 1984 shattered our dreams. The way Sikhs were massacred in cold blood, we lost confidence in the Hindu-majority Government of India. Our family felt that anything could happen to minorities any time. So we decided to migrate to Canada.' Three of the four brothers live in Canada and one lives in the United States. Nav's father sold his business and home in Green Park and moved in with his sons to Canada. He lived with Nav and his wife, Arvinder until he died in 1998. Nav and his wife have a special room for keeping the *Guru Granth Sahib.*

'I learnt the Sikh way of life right from my childhood. My parents were honest, hard-working and religious people.'

'What was your first job in this country?' I asked Nav.

'Car sales,' Nav replied. 'The employer first refused to hire me because of my turban. I asked him to give me a chance. As luck would have it, he was in need and called me a few days later.' Nav was so successful in selling that he was soon made the General Manager of the branch.

'My employer discovered that the company was losing heavily in this particular area. I turned it around in one year's time and showed a profit of two and a half million dollars. It wasn't long before I was able buy him out. I am now the sole owner of this company.'

I asked Nav to tell me about his involvement in social activities.

'In 1995 I started sponsoring cultural shows for South Asians in classy places such as community halls and theatres normally visited by the whites. This was not to make money for myself, but to let the whites know that we Sikhs amount to something.'

'Why do you think we need to prove something to the whites? Did anything happen?' I asked.

'Yes something did. I had gone to see a gora sahib in this country. He saw me emerging from a taxi and took me to be a cab driver. That hurt me—not that there is anything wrong in being a cab driver, but there was something inadmissible about his believing that all Sikhs are cab drivers. Instead of getting angry, I made a resolve to go some day and sit in places where the most *rayees* sit. I wanted to see Sikhs occupying the centre stage of life in my adopted country,' explained Nav.

He told us how he bought his first ticket to a basketball game; how he spends fifty to sixty thousand dollars every years just to watch basketball games. He buys front row tickets and TV cameras are usually focused on him. He has become a bigger star than some of the players, and has become such a celebrity that people want to shake hands with him and have their pictures taken with him.

'It takes me over an hour to walk out of a game,' he explained. 'People line up to have a word with me. It is all due to my turban.' He touched his light grey turban with both his hands.

Now the Raptors Basketball Team has made it a practice to let Nav start the game.

'An elephant brings the ball to me, so I get to throw the first ball,' continued Nav. 'This is the biggest honour bestowed on a common citizen like me.'

Nav has started sponsoring a Baisakhi Day Game every year

Over 5,000 tickets are sold to Asian viewers, and millions of people watch the event on television. Sikhs perform *gatka, bhangra* and *giddha,* while turbaned Sikh policemen and hundreds of turbaned youngsters look on.

Nav does not visit India as often as he would like to. He occasionally accompanies his wife, who visits her parents in New Delhi every year. Nav wants his daughter to stay in touch with Indian culture and visit important gurdwaras in Punjab.

Nav is not very clear about his views on the demand for a separate Sikh State. He says, 'Every movement is born of some injustice done to someone. In a business partnership, if someone is not getting a fair deal, she or he will want to separate. When Pakistan was created we Sikhs thought we could get justice from a Hindu-majority government. We were wrong. I am a lay man, I cannot comment on the feasibility of the creation of Khalistan. But I want a country where Sikhs are safe, where they can be productive, and can prosper.'

He continued, 'I am not a learned man, but in my humble way I am trying to do something for the community. In the recent past I took the Mayor of this city to court, because she said some derogatory things about South Asian Women visiting a local hospital in their native clothing. The Health Minister happens to be a friend and I told him that I intended to sue the Mayor of Toronto. She could not sleep for nights, and tried to pacify me. But I did not relent till she apologized,' said Nav with joy and pride.

A little later, he left for his office while I settled down to talk to his wife and daughter.

Arvinder, Nav's wife enjoys her role as a housewife, and does not miss those days of independence when she worked in New Delhi at Escorts. She is happy that she can look after her husband's needs, and spend a lot of time with her only child—her eleven-year-old daughter, Kudrat. She takes care of her mother-in-law as well. But her life seems to revolve around her daughter. 'I stay involved in all her activities; I help her with her homework, I take her to Punjabi classes; now that summer is fast approaching I don't want her to watch television all day, I will take her to her friends—Indian and Canadians. And I will see to it that she is busy doing something constructive, learning something new.'

Once when Kudrat's friends asked her why she didn't cut her hair, she replied, 'It's against the law!' Her mother laughed, then explained to her that it wasn't against the law, but against her religion. Kudrat knows Punjabi and recites the opening lines of the morning prayer and a few hymns.

The last person I met in the house was Nav's mother. She spends most of her time in her room either reading Punjabi newspapers and magazines, or in prayer. She is eighty-five years old, but as fit as a fiddle. She tells me that in her youth she used to write for *Preet-lari,* Punjabi weekly started by Gurbax Singh of Preet Nagar.

That was the highlight of my visit to Nav's home. I thought of Khalil Gibran's line: 'Show me your mother's face and I will tell you who you are.' (Khalil Gibran in *Spiritual Sayings of Khalil Gibran.*)

CANADA

Lawyer With an Edge

T-SHER SINGH

T-Sher Singh's family came out of Pakistan as refugees and made Patna their home. They left a flourishing business in auto spare parts and migrated to Canada. He is now the leading lawyer in Guelph, and had the guts to take the Prime Minister of Canada to court.

Canada is a country of vast lands, peace, beauty and calm. Driving in the early hours of the morning on broad highways bereft of traffic was a blissful experience. We turned into a small township and looked for T-Sher Singh's office and residence, and found it without any difficulty. My companion directed me to a place where T-Sher Singh ate breakfast everyday—a hotel-cum-restaurant managed by Punjabis who had recently immigrated from Scotland. It was a fabulous treat of parathas, pickles and vegetables with T-Sher Singh.

T-Sher Singh then took us to his apartment. We passed a room in which I could see the *Guru Granth Sahib*—his library—on our way to his sitting room. I couldn't keep my eyes off the beautiful paintings, sculptures, and rare pieces of art that adorned the walls and the tables.

T-Sher Singh was born and brought up in Patna—the capital of the eastern state of Bihar. His parents came from Jehlam, and Rawalpindi, both now in Pakistan. They had to flee their home in 1947 during the violence that erupted following India's Independence and Partition. T-Sher Singh's family lost all they had including a number of relatives during the mass exodus. His parents, alongwith the surviving brothers, decided to make their new home in Patna, where they and their extended family started a business in auto spare parts. 'Sher' as he likes to be addressed, was born in 1949 and was named Tapisher Singh. His parents called him 'Sher'. It is a name he has learnt to like, and he has retained the initial 'T' from Tapisher.

Sher was two-and-a-half years old when his father took him to a kindergarten school run by Irish nuns. The nuns looked after him even after school was over. This school was like his castle surrounded by lakes and ponds and rolling hills.

When he was seven years old, he was sent to a boarding school away from home. While he was the eldest of five children, he ended up as the youngest boy in his class. His classmates called him 'Baby Singh', and often bullied him. Left with little choice he had to learn to fight back, and thus developed his Sher (lion) like aggressiveness.

Often he felt lonely and looked for opportunities to return home. But his father made sure that Sher stayed where he was, so that he could devote all his time to studies.

The family business picked up rapidly. All seemed to be going well till, in the 1960s, the family felt the impact of civil unrest in India. They were again an affluent minority in the poorest state of India.

'It was time to move again... maybe to the Western world,' said Sher. He was about twenty years old, and didn't complete his college degree because college exams were postponed due to mob violence on the campus.

After visiting forty different countries, Sher's parents decided to settle in Canada.

T-Sher Singh being awarded an honorary Doctor of Law degree by the Chancellor of Lakehead University, Canada, at its Annual Convention in 1998.

T-Sher Singh in conversation with His Holiness, Pope John Paul II, at the Vatican in 1999.

'It looked like a place where there was little conflict, and if there were any, they were resolved in a very civilized way,' said Sher.

The extended family moved to Canada in 1971, the year when Sher enrolled at Lakehead University in Thunder Bay, Ontario.

'There was this feeling that there were no limits to what you could do. That was a very important feeling to have as a young person starting out in life,' said Sher. But after completing a Master's degree in English, Sher had to spend many years doing odd jobs like delivering newspapers, and working as a security guard. Then he got a job as a troubleshooter in a brokerage house.

'There was a terrible sense of frustration. My brothers and I were not being used to our full potential,' said Sher.

In 1974, Sher returned to India and married a Sikh girl of his choice. This marriage did not last long. From that marriage, Sher has a daughter, Gehna Kaur.

After much soul-searching, he decided to opt for Law. On his thirtieth birthday, married and with a baby, he put his condominium up for sale, and decided to move to the University of Western Ontario to study Law. His troubles were far from over! The Law School refused to accept his Indian university degree. It took him two years to convince people at the Law School that his qualifications were as good as the local ones:

Finally, two years later, in 1980 the University of Western Ontario accepted him and a whole new world opened up for him. Although his marriage fell apart, he got custody of his three-year-old daughter.

Sher refers to his years at the University of Western Ontario as the golden years when he was treated by his peers and professors with respect, because he was a fast learner, and Law really fascinated him.

Sher was elected President of the Student Body of the Law

School. He also became the founder and editor of the yearbook of the graduating class of the Law School at the University of Western Ontario. After finishing completing Law School, he started looking for a job. Every firm he applied to responded favourably without bothering about his turban and beard.

He is best known for his action against the former Prime Minister Martin Brian Mulroney for appointing Nova Scotia Premier John Buchanan to the Senate, while Buchanan was being interrogated by the RCMP (Royal Canadian Mounted Police) on charges of corruption. Mulroney appointed eight new senators for the express purpose of pushing through the controversial legislation to establish Goods and Service Tax. Sher called it 'stacking' and took him to court.

Sher's widely publicized lawsuit was no surprise to observers of Canadian origin, but the High Commissioner of India took Sher aside at a party and asked him, 'What on earth made you take on the Prime Minister? Did you think you could win?'

Sher did not win the case, but was able to send a message to all Canadians—they too had a right to demand accountability from their elected representatives.

At the age of fifty-one, T-Sher Singh has a flourishing practice at Guelph, Ontario. He chose the small town over Toronto because life in Toronto had become very hectic. 'There is a certain amount of decency in a small town,' he says.

During 1990–1993, Sher served on the Ontario Police Commission, which oversees policy and standards of the 120 municipal police forces in the province. A year before his appointment, he was a member of the Ontario Task Force on Policing and Race Relations. Its report led to sweeping changes in policing in Ontario. He has chaired the Council of Policing and Race Relations, and also has served on the Board of Directors of the Metro Toronto Children's Aid Society and the Urban Alliance on Race Relations.

He is a frequent TV and Radio commentator on various national networks, and has from time to time, appeared as a regular panelist on a number of shows. He recently hosted a weekly (13 part) TV talk show on Sikh issues and perspectives entitled *'Sat Siri Akaal'* with his daughter Gehna Kaur; he appeared each week on another 26-part TV series, '*Conversations on Sikhism.*' He has also produced three documentary videos: *Sikh Canadians: The Promise and the Challenge, The Golden Temple of Amritsar* and *Ranjit Singh: Emperor of Punjab.* In 1987, he produced the Governor General's Award winner Sharon Pollock's play *The Komagata Maru Incident,* at a downtown Toronto theatre, and in London, Ontario.

Although Sher had started writing when he was a boy in India, it is only in the past ten years that he has taken to it seriously. Now he is a regular columnist on current issues in the *Toronto Star,* and the *Guelph Mercury.* He writes a weekly travel column for the *Kitchener Waterloo Record.* His travel column is picked up by various other papers. He is the author of articles on various issues ranging from Law and Justice, Policing, Religion, Sikhism to Race Relations, Human Rights and Civil Liberties. He also lectures on these topics from coast to coast in North America. Sher also writes a regular column for www.sikhe.com, the primary online Sikh 'newspaper'.

Sher makes it a point to travel to different countries seven to eight times a year and has so far visited fifty countries. His varied interests, life experiences and an optimistic outlook provide him the material for his newspaper columns and television broadcasts.

In 1997, he spearheaded the celebrations of the Centennial of the first Sikh Settlement in Canada. Again in 1999, he was part of the vanguard of the Canadian celebrations of the Baisakhi Tricentenary, and was involved in the approval, design and issuance of the Canada Post Commemorative stamp released on 19 April marking the Centennial and the Tricentenary. In recognition of his contributions, Sher was awarded the degree of Doctor of Law, *honoris causa,* by

Lakehead University, Thunder Bay, Onatrio, Canada in May 1998. Earlier in 1990, the year he moved to Guelph, he was selected its Newsmaker of the Year.

More recently, in October 1999, Sher was invited by the Vatican to participate (as one of the 200 delegates of different faiths from around the world) in a week-long interfaith assembly held in the Vatican, to mark the commencement of The Great Jubilee Celebrations at the turn of the new millennium. Following the invitation, Sher spoke to other members of the local Sikh community about presenting a gift to the Vatican. He did not waste any time and contracted a renowned sculptor and asked if he would be interested in producing a sculpture, which would eventually be placed beside the works of Michelangelo. Sculptor Hugh Russel produced the sculpture, entitled 'The Column of Brotherhood'—an Ionic column with figures on each side representing a Catholic priest and a Sikh. A detailed report written by Scott Tracey regarding this event appeared in the *Guelph Mercury* showing a picture of the sculpture depicting Catholic and Sikh men and women linking arms in unity and support. Sher carried it to the Vatican where he met Pope John Paul II, and helped unveil the bronze sculpture.

Sher used to visit India regularly, but now that all members of his extended family are in Canada his visits have become less frequent. He says, 'This is home. I thrive on the freedom this country offers, I like to prove to myself that I have civic rights and duties. Also I did certain things, because I felt the Sikh community here did not have a voice. Now that the younger generation is taking over, I feel relieved, I can travel and write.'

He is a single parent of his only child Gehna Kaur. 'I do not want to impose Indian culture on her. I am happy about her being a Canadian. I want her to retain her Sikh identity. She is learning what it takes to be a Sikh.' Gehna Kaur is twenty and is studying media journalism.

'What kind of a man is she likely to marry?'

'I would like her to a marry a Sikh, but I encourage her to date even outside the community.'

T. Sher Singh does not mince his words talking about Sikh leaders. He says, 'I cannot think of a single one who deserves my respect. But I have great faith in our youth. Somebody will emerge. No one had heard of Ranjit Singh in 1788, and in 1789 he emerged on the scene in a big way.

'Punjab is in a mess, leaders are crooks, but we are facing a larger issue of survival. The local politics of Punjab is not important. I am referring to the leaders at the national level in Indian politics. Sikhs were always the nation builders and the saviours, but look at them now!' He pronounces his views on the demand for a separate state for the Sikhs. 'Khalistan was never a movement. It was something that came out of extreme distress in a country that the Sikhs had helped liberate and build, in a society that turned against them. That idea took birth among some Sikhs but I don't think they ever wanted a Khalistan.'

In January 2000, T-Sher Singh was appointed a member of the Order of Canada for Volunteerism—the first Sikh to be so honoured with the country's most prestigious award.

CANADA

Leading the Toronto Sikh Community

HARBHAJAN SINGH PANDORI

I had met Harbhajan Singh Pandori very briefly in 1994 when I happened to be in Toronto. When I revisited Toronto to interview him, he had just lost his mother. It was an occasion on which I was able to see some of the bonding which held the community together. Almost the entire Sikh community of Toronto was present at the crematorium. The following day I went to the house where the Akhand Paath was going on. The house was full of people. Some sat in the main room listening to the Akhand Paath, while others were helping in the kitchen. As the sun went down, the mood became more religious and subdued but there was nothing sad or tragic about it.

The Pandoris are a unique family. They came to Canada three decades ago, and have sponsored over forty relatives from Punjab to migrate to Canada. They have invested in estates and own large houses in Canada.

When I inquired about his surname Pandori, Harbhajan Singh replied, 'We are Ghumans from a village named Pandori. When I was in grade school, our teacher could not distinguish

Harbhajan Singh Pandori with his wife Surinder, their son Paul and their two daughters Amrit and Simran.

Harbhajan Singh Pandori with David Peterson, Former Premier of Ontario.

between so many Ghumans, so he addressed me by the name of my village Pandori. General Mohan Singh of the INA was also a Ghuman. We gave all our savings to him to be passed on to Netaji Subhash Chandra Bose.'

Pandori has four younger brothers and two sisters. All of them live in Canada. As a child he was good at studies and a topper in his class. After finishing High School from his village, he had to cycle a long distance each day to attend National College (now known as Guru Tegh Bahadur Government College) at Sathiala. On graduating he moved to Chandigarh to get a Master's degree in Economics.

Pandori first tried his luck in Hong Kong where his grandfather had been living for some decades. But he did not like the claustrophobic environment in Hong Kong and returned to India. His next choice was Canada. In 1970 he came to Toronto. Once in Toronto, he cut off his long hair and shaved his beard in order to get a good job. But having done that, he felt so bad that he had high fever for many days. So he grew his hair and beard back again. Soon he got a job as a security guard. Along with the job he studied to be a school teacher.

'At that time Canada needed teachers and I was able to get a scholarship to qualify as a teacher in this country,' said Pandori. Ever since, he has taught in schools and has enrolled himself in some study programme or the other, to stay abreast of technological developments, especially in Computer Science.

In 1973 he went back to India and married Surinder whom he had met at a cousin's wedding. He is happy with Surinder (he called her Chindo) and they have a son, Paul, and two daughters, Amrit and Simran, all in their twenties. The daughters are doing well. Amrit has a good job in a stock exchange company in its Communications Department, and Simran is studying English Literature at the university. Paul, now twenty-six, has developed an identity crisis. He was the only Sikh boy in his class with long hair tied up in a jura and covered with a patka. Unable to bear peer pressure, he went and got his hair cut without his parents' consent. Ever since, he has lost interest in his studies. I sensed that it was extremely painful for the parents to talk about the plight of their first-born, their only son.

I asked Harbhajan Pandori about his involvement in the community affairs, and his role as President of what is said to be the largest ever gurdwara in the world. He replied that he was involved in the affairs of the gurdwara in his village and took a keen interest in the activities of his college at Chandigarh. His involvement got stronger in 1984 after Operation Bluestar. He was pained by the fact that despite the tragedy, the management of the Dixie Road Gurdwara continued to bicker and fight amongst themselves over small matters.

'My friends realized my pain and frustration, and decided to encourage me to take the matters of the gurdwara in my hands. I was elected President of the Dixie Road Gurdwara in 1985 and continue to be so to date.'

In December 1987 Harbhajan Pandori took amrit and became a full-fledged Khalsa. Wearing a kirpan, part of the five mandatory K's, however, has landed him in troublesome situations in his hometown, Toronto, and overseas, in India. In Toronto he used to teach Punjabi to Sikh students. Some of these students started wearing kirpans over their shirts. When questioned, they replied, 'If our teacher Mr Pandori can wear a kirpan, why can't we?' So Mr Pandori was asked to stop wearing his kirpan by the Superintendent of the Peel Board of Education—a case that he fought in court for years, and won. The victory brought him publicity, and credit to his community.

During his travels around the world, he had never had trouble because of his kirpan, till the day he reached the Indira Gandhi International Airport at New Delhi. There security officers took off his kirpan promising to deliver it to him at his next destination. That, however, never happened.

'That kirpan,' said Pandori, 'was smaller than the knives given to passengers to carve meat served on board. I don't know why Indians want to humiliate us, why they want to deprive us of our symbols'

I changed the subject and asked him about the gurdwara over which he presided. 'Our gurdwara can accommodate 80,000 people at a time. We have, at any given point twelve to sixteen raagi jathas residing in our premises, waiting for their turn to perform kirtan in the Sunday diwans. There was a time they went around in the city shopping malls wearing jeans and making fools of themselves in their half-Punjabi, half-Western outfits, trying to kill time during the weekdays. I requested them to start doing kirtan in the gurdwara (each jatha would have to be on duty for about one hour each day). They refused to do so, saying that would be a waste of time because during the week there was hardly any sangat. I told them sangat will start coming once there was kirtan in the gurdwara. Finally I had to give them an ultimatum, and told them that I would have them sent back to Punjab if they refused to comply. Now we have kirtan from 5 a.m. to 9 p.m. People bring their newborn babies for the Guru's blessings and give money to these raagis. If someone buys a new car, he comes to the gurdwara first and gives money to the raagis. Now everyone is happy.'

'How did you presume that sangat would come to the gurdwara during the week' I asked.

'*Bhainji*, there is a lot of *shraddha* amongst the Sikhs of the city. There are many elderly people doing nothing at home. They come to the gurdwara to do sewa and listen to kirtan. But it took a little time getting things going. I had to go to the gurdwara at 5 a.m. get these raagis started with Asa di war, then in the evening get a *granthi* to do the *Rehras Path.*

'How many people visit the gurdwara every week?'

'Normally there are between 8,000–10,000 people but on special occasions like the Gurpurab, the sangat can go upto

80,000 people. On such occasions we remove the partitions. There is a sea of humanity in one big hall with the *Guru Granth Sahib* on an elevated platform.'

'What about the education of the children?'

'On an average we have 700 to 800 children learning Gurmukhi and kirtan from qualified instructors on the payroll of the gurdwara. And did you know that Punjabi is one of the elective subjects in Canada's schools, and there are about 8,000 students from all races learning Gurmukhi in Canadian schools? Some enroll in these classes held in the evenings, or over the weekends. My own daughters have studied Punjabi as a second language upto grade 12 in their schools.'

'Talking about your daughters, will they marry someone from the Sikh community, or...?'

'I want my daughters to marry within the community, but then I have to prepare myself for anything that they might decide to do. If they decide to marry a white or Hindu, I will not be too upset. But I cannot understand why I feel I will not be able to accept a Muslim as a member of my family. I have thought about it, especially as I do have many Muslim friends.'

Pandori was outspoken about his support for Khalistan.

'We Sikhs need our own country where we can practice our religion freely. The way the Hindu-majority government treats us is very unfair. If only they would treat us with respect and affection, we would do anything for our country. It is like this—if you treat a woman with love and affection, she will bear you twenty children willingly, but if you try to rape her, she will land you in jail. Our Sikh community has been raped by the rulers of India, and we can't even take them to court. Now the Government of India is speaking so highly of Mahajara Ranjit Singh. Why doesn't the government treat us and other minorities in India the same way that Maharaja Ranjit Singh treated his people?' There was more hurt than anger in Harbhajan Singh Pandori's voice.

He told me that last year he went to India after twenty years.

The treatment meted out to him at the airport in New Delhi did not come as a surprise. But his agony was far from over. When he went to his village, he saw men distilling liquor in their homes and women selling it by the roadside. 'Disgraceful!'

His daughter Amrit walked in as we were winding up the interview and spoke to me about certain concerns of the younger generation of Sikhs in Canada. Simran, the younger sister, joined us as well. They were both torn between their personal desires and social values at large. Most parents are usually worried about their image in society, and especially among the relatives they have brought to Canada. I asked Amrit if it means something to her to be a Sikh.

'It means a lot,' she replied. 'We just lost our grandmother. At such a time, if we didn't have the community here, if we didn't have a gurdwara, our family would have gone crazy. It is good to know that we are a part of a community.'

CANADA

Building Bridges

GURDIP SINGH SALUJA

Putting it down to a rough estimate, there are around 500,000 Sikhs, and 115 gurdwaras in Canada. The earliest immigrants made their homes in British Columbia where the majority still live.

Gurdip made Canada his home in 1975. Like other immigrant Sikhs, he faced discrimination when he was looking for a job. Even so he was able to get a job as a Mechanical Engineer. After several years in that profession, he chose to become a real estate agent in 1987. He was doing voluntary work with a charitable organization called The American Sikh League when he was appointed as Chairperson of the Employment Insurance Board of Referees for the district of Brampton. This is a prestigious appointment by the Governor General in Council. Gurdip has been reappointed for the third consecutive term.

Gurdip was born on 25 May 1945 in Rawalpindi, now in Pakistan. Gurdip's father, Sardar Arjan Singh was a teacher who later served as Vice Principal at Gujranwala Guru Nanak

Gurdip Singh Saluja with his wife Darshan, their daughter Monica and their sons Inderpal and Sarabjit.

Gurdip Singh Saluja with Prime Minister Jean Chretien at a gathering.

Khalsa College, in Ludhiana. He has written several book on Mathematics. Gurdip's brother, Sardar Amarjit Singh Deepak, now settled in Chandigarh, has been a top executive with the Mahindra group of companies.

Gurdip completed his education in Mechanical Engineering in India, and married Darshan, the daughter of Sardar Harnam Singh Ahluwalia, Deputy Director of Vigilance in the Punjab Government. Their elder son, Inderpal was just over a year old when they migrated to Canada. Inderpal did very well in his studies and completed his Master's degree in Medicine in 2001.

Gurdip and Darshan had to struggle to get their first jobs. Darshan was lucky to start out as a draftsperson. Over the years she has proved her worth, and is now working in a senior position with a leading construction company. Gurdip had to settle for a Shipper Receiver's post to survive until he got his professional engineer's designation. His decision to keep his hair and turban made things more difficult. He got a rude shock when one of the prospective employers bluntly told him that the job could be his if he 'Canadianized' himself. He refused the offer and waited till he found the right employer.

Gurdip and Darshan were blessed with two more children—Sarabjit and Monica. Sarabjit has just completed his Master's degree in Business Administration, and is working in a managerial position with Bell Canada. Monica is a bright young lady who is in the final year of her High School.

Gurdip says that getting used to the ways of the new country has not been easy. They got used to the weather quite soon, which was perhaps the easiest part. There were lots of other adjustments to be made. Inderpal and Sarabjit with their unshorn hair and patkas covering their heads were probably the most visible members of the minorities in their schools. They were picked upon and roughed up but refused to go under. They had to do well in their studies, sports and extra-curricular activities to get accepted. Then there was the co-mingling of two cultures, which proved to be the hardest for the family. They still feel the occasional culture shock. The real challenge of living in a bicultural if not multicultural society presented itself when their eldest son Inderpal decided to court Jennifer, a Christian of Scottish descent. They were married in August 2001 with their parents' blessings.

AUSTRALIA

Singer with a Mission

DYA SINGH

A granthi's son born in Malaysia, trained to be a Chartered Accountant in England, turned into a rock singer of the Gurbani in Australia and now performs all over the world—that's Dya Singh for you.

It must have been the coldest night of the year. I was at Princeton Railway Station waiting for my brother Harjit to pick me up, and could only see a vast stretch of snow.

Harjit finally arrived forty-five minutes late. I got into his car without a word. Instead of apologizing for keeping me waiting in the cold, he turned on his car stereo and we were back on the road. I turned a deaf ear to the music.

'Listen to this CD,' he pleaded. 'I do so on my way to work, so does Sunny (Sandeep, his son). Do you know the singer? Dya Singh. He explains everything in English. Just listen to his powerful voice, and hear the instruments playing in the background.' I straightened up, listened and forgave my brother for keeping me waiting.

Time flies and sometimes we forget even the most memorable

moments. Similarly years went by without hearing the voice of the singer I had heard in my brother's car.

Late in June last year, I received a call from a lady named Satwant, a friend of Dya Singh.

'I am calling to let you know that Dya Singh of Australia is going to sing at a church near your place. I am sure you know who Dya Singh is. He has formed the World Music Group that has emerged as one of the most sought after music groups in Australia, Southeast Asia, the United States and Canada.'

Then came a flyer from Satwant giving specific information about the time, date and place where the proposed concert was going to be held. With it she had attached quotations of what had been written about him.

'Dya Singh's incredible voice amazed me, at times quietly sensitive, at others overwhelmingly powerful, and always with the pure melody.' (Barbara Roberts, *InFOLKus Magazine.)*

With the production of Dya Singh's highly acclaimed CD *300* which won Dya Singh the award for Male Artist of the Year at the World Music Awards held in Sydney, Australia in March 2000, Dya Singh has become a household name in the multicultural World Music.

I decided to find out more about this legendary man. I followed the ladies clad in salwar kameezes and the men in turbans to the church that I had not seen before. It was packed. On the stage was a group of musicians. Dya Singh was wearing a black shirt, blacks trousers and a black turban. Accompanying him were a tabla player, with shoulder-length hair, a pretty young girl, his daughter Hersal Kaur in her salwar kameez, and two young men as white as they could be. Dya Singh introduced them to the audience.

Then he started with *Jaap* of *Sat Naam*. After that he introduced his latest CD on the Sukhmani, and sang, '*Aad Gur-e-Nameh, Jugad Gue-e-Nameh*' and went on to sing several of his favourite pieces from the Sukhmani.

Dya Singh with his elder brother Gurmukh Singh, after receiving the Sword of Honour, in London.

Dya Singh spreading the message of the Guru through song. Accompanying him on his mission are his youngest daughter Praveen Kaur and his tabla player.

The next day I went to see Dya Singh. He was still in his black outfit, friendly and willing to talk.

'Since I am taking the Gurbani to a larger public, it is going to cause a lot of controversy. I am going to tread on many toes. Professional raagis are looking for opportunities to shoot me down. One gurdwara president called me the other day and asked me if the whites in my audiences dance to my tunes, when I sing the Gurbani.' Then Dya Singh talked about the previous night after he had sung the Gurbani, he sang one of Nusrat Fateh Ali Khan's '*Dham Mast Mast.*'

'Religious prudes—*dharma de thekedar* will no doubt want to put an end to my singing.'

'What do you think you are doing?' I asked.

'I am taking the message of Sikhism to the younger generation and to the multicultural audiences worldwide. Naturally there are traditionalists who frown upon my novel approach.'

Dya Singh was born on Baisakhi day in 1950, in a small town called Raub in Malaysia. He is the youngest of four children. He has two elder brothers and a sister. The eldest brother, Gurmukh Singh lives in London and had just retired from British Civil Service. He is Dya Singh's mentor. After their father's death, Dya Singh looked upon Gurmukh Singh as a father figure. The other brother, Baldev Singh also lives in Australia and is a qualified civil engineer. His sister lives in San Jose, California with her family. They rarely visit India.

Dya Singh's father Giani Harchand Singh and mother Bibi Mohinder Kaur hailed from a village named Rai Kot Bassian near Moga in Punjab. His father was a granthi of the regiment's gurdwara in Ambala cantonment. He was transferred to Malaysia as the granthi of the gurdwara in Raub. Dya Singh has some painful memories of his father being mistreated by the gurdwara management committee.

'Now the same thing is happening to me. Some of these gurdwara presidents tell me that I cannot do kirtan in a gurdwara because I have a Hindu tabla player. I don't have to depend on gurdwaras to carry out my mission. I have an audience everywhere I go.'

I asked about his schooling.

'I went to Muslim schools in Malaysia and have a special affinity with Muslims. I can say Namaaz with ease and clarity,' he declared with a gleam in his eye.

Dya Singh's father migrated to England in 1971. Dya Singh continued his education in England and graduated as a chartered account. He worked as an accountant for several years in England before migrating to Australia in 1981 because his employer moved his business there. While still in England, he once again met Jasbir Kaur who was a psychiatric nurse who had been his sweetheart since his schooldays in Malaysia. He married Jasbir in 1973. They have three daughters—Jamel Kaur (twenty-five), Hersal Kaur (eighteen), and Praveen Kaur (fifteen).

Dya Singh started reminiscing, 'Love for the Gurbani and *sangeet* was instilled in all of us by our bapuji right from our childhood. The multicultural environment in Malaysia also proved beneficial. As a child I was fond of singing Tamil and Malay songs. Neighbours used to gather around in the evening to listen to my singing. At the time I was encouraged by the gurdwara sangat whenever I did *Shabad Kirtan.*'

Dya Singh and Keith Preston formed a music group, and performed at folk festivals in Australia. The state government of south Australia sent them to the Singapore Arts Festival. It was reported in the press that a Khalsa was doing kirtan in the malls where thousands of Chinese and others were standing around listening. A newspaper reported the event as 'a unique blend of mystical North Indian music with Western folk… that has captivated everyone who has heard it.'

The group was invited by the local gurdwaras in Singapore to perform kirtan. It was a tremendous success. The group went to Japan on a cultural exchange programme. It performed a series of eleven concerts. A Japanese interpreter had come to Australia some months earlier and translated twenty shabads into Japanese. Dya Singh received e-mail from several Indian Sikhs and Japanese telling him that a lot of Japanese pilgrims were visiting the Golden Temple in Amritsar.

'How do you people sustain yourselves? I mean financially?' I asked.

'We get contracts for festivals, art festivals, world music festivals, and we produce CDs for sale. New sponsors are coming forward, and we treat these contacts as business proposals.' He went on to add, 'I have gone through very rough times in the course of moving from accounting to music. Now my manager Keith Preston is a very astute person, and handles finances very well. We get our salaries on time. Even my daughters draw a salary, and they have their own bank accounts.'

My first question after eating a hearty meal was about his daily routine.

'I like to get up before sunrise, because I enjoy my *Naam Simran* at dawn. I like to look at the rising sun as it changes its colour and spreads its rays. I am a tea man. I drink lots of tea in the morning and don't eat anything other than fruit throughout the morning. I do my *riaz* early in the morning. My bapuji had taught us that you truly sing the Gurbani when your soul is singing with you. Without your soul, you sing mechanically. I normally write a shabad, translate it, then come up with a raga that will give it a twenty-first century relevance.

'My lunch is haphazard. I like to take a nap between 2.30 p.m. and 3 p.m. in the afternoon. I exercise in the evening. Either I go for a long walk or play a game of tennis. At night I open my e-mail. I get about half a dozen e-mail from youngsters. Sikhs around the world ask questions about Sikhism or my music. I write back immediately.'

In the evening I do Rehras and *Kirtan Sohila.* I have taken amrit and consider myself a Khalsa. Nobody can take that away from me. I do eat meat, because the Rehat Maryada allows it. I do not drink any more.'

'Did your daughters have any problems going to school in Australia?'

'We are a tiny minority in Adelaide. Some Sikh children are embarrassed about their fathers coming to school to pick them up, but not my daughters. Whenever it was my turn to pick them up from school, they would tell everyone "Daddy" is coming. Many people ask me how I have such rapport with my children. I spend time with them. Sikh parents should make their children feel proud of their heritage. I have gone as far as visiting my daughter's school. In front of the class, I have taken off my turban, let my long hair down, then retied my hair and turban in front of the class. Just to show them who I am and tell them why I keep my hair long and my beard unshorn. My daughters have never faced any problems because of being Sikhs.'

'What do you think is your biggest achievement in life?'

'Taking the Gurbani to the younger generation. My most enjoyable moment is one when a youngster comes to me and says, "Uncle I never liked kirtan, but now I listen to you every day." Then mothers come to me and say, "The children have dragged us to gurdwara because of you."

'Once a kid told his father, "When Uncle Dya Singh gets on the stage, *kuch kuch hota hai* (something happens)." '

Dya Singh feels there is too much of corruption in the SGPC and the Akali Party. Gurdwaras under the SGPC are not working well.

'And I have not heard anything sensible coming out of the SGPC. Even the Jathedar of the Akal Takht issues *hukum namas* single-handedly on the basis of his own whims and fancies. Decisions should be made collectively. Not all the five Takhts should be based in India. There should be one each in London, the United States, Kenya, and Australia. Sikhism is a religion of the future.

'The gurdwara committees that are elected for one year are not feasible because, once elected, instead of doing any constructive work for the gurdwara members, start thinking about how to win the next election in order to stay in power. A police officer in Southall said to me that when national elections take place, there is peace and harmony, but whenever gurdwara elections take place, the police are deployed everywhere.'

Glossary

akhand paath	continuous recitation of the *Guru Granth Sahib*
amrit vela	early morning, considered the blessed hour
amrit	nectar
amritdhari	one who has partaken of *amrit* and strictly observes the *rehat maryada* and other injunctions in his daily life and conduct
ardas	supplication to the Supreme One
asa di war	literally a ballad of hope; a section of the *Guru Granth Sahib*
bapuji	father
bhainjee	sister
bhangra	Punjabi folk dance
bua	father's sister
chardi kala	the inspiring spirit of the Sikhs which affirms positive and firm belief in the bright side of life and the ever-rising spirit
chhole bhature	savoury chickpeas with puffed wheat bread
daal	Punjabi dish prepared with lentils and spices
daswandh	literally one-tenth; a contribution in cash or in kind of one-tenth of a Sikh's earnings to the Guru to be spent on projects or activities of the community
dharma de thekedar	keepers of religion
dharma prachar	spreading the message of the Gurus
diwan	literally Royal Court; Sikh religious service
dupatta	long scarf
gatka	form of Punjabi martial arts

giddha	Punjabi folk dance
gora sahib	white gentleman
gora	white
granthi	priest; man or woman with a whisk, in attendance of the *Guru Granth Sahib* at a gurdwara
gurbani	literally the voice of the Gurus; writings of the Gurus in the *Guru Granth Sahib*
gurmat	resolution adopted in the presence of the *Guru Granth Sahib*
gurmukhi	the script in which the *Guru Granth Sahib* has been written, now also the official Punjabi script
guru ka langar	the Guru's kitchen
hukum nama	instructions of the Gurus or edicts issued by members of Sikh authority
ishnan	bath
jaap	recitation
jagir	landholding
japji sahib	morning prayer composed by Guru Nanak
jatha	group
jootee	Indian hand-stitched footwear
jura	hair tied up in a knot
kara	steel bangle
keshdhari	one who in addition to observing the basic Sikh beliefs and practices, wears his hair uncut and his beard unshaven
khalsa panth	order of the pure
khalsa	literally the pure
kirpan	sword/dagger
kirtan sohila	final hymn sung every night before the *Guru Granth Sahib* is 'put to bed'
kirtan	hymn singing
kurta pajama	Indian dress comprising a loose shirt and trousers
langar	kitchen; free meal
mathian	savoury snack
nagar kirtan	chanting of the Gurbani as the *Guru Granth Sahib* placed on a decorated vehicle led by the *Panj Piyare* (five beloved ones), is taken out in a procession.
naam simran	recitation of the Name of the Lord
nishan-e-khalsa	honour bestowed on distinguished Sikhs by the Akal Takht; the emblem of the Sikh faith

palak paneer	popular Punjabi dish prepared with spinach and cottage cheese
parikarma	circumambulatory pathway around a holy shrine
paath	reading of the *Guru Granth Sahib*
patka	piece of cloth tied on the hair before the turban is worn
pauri	step
pehelwan	wrestler
pind	village/homeland
pugri	turban
raagi jathas	hymn singers at a gurdwara
rayees	wealthy person
rehat maryada	code of conduct
rehras paath	recitation of the evening prayer
rehras	evening prayer
riaz	practice especially for music
rishta	relation; marriage proposal
sadhana	meditation
sahjdhari	one who believes in and follows the essentials of the Sikh faith
salwar kameez	Punjabi dress
samagam	religious assembly
sangat	congregation
sangeet	music
sarbat khalsa	representative assembly of Sikhs
saropa	robe or token of honour; usually a piece of cloth to be tied as a turban, or worn as a scarf over the shoulders
sat nam	the Name of the Lord
satguruji	the Almighty
sewa	service dedicated to the community
sewadars	volunteers at a gurdwara
shabad kirtan	singing of religious hymns from the *Guru Granth Sahib*
shabad vaak	recitation of the first couplet on a page of the *Guru Granth Sahib* opened at random
shabad	religious hymn
shraddha	faith; reverence
Sikh suba	Sikh heartland
simran	remembrance of the Lord
sukhmani sahib	poetical composition by Guru Arjan Dev
thathaa	piece of cloth tied over the beard to fix it in place